Been There, Done that
...Happy Dance!

Sharon Canfield Dorsey

Copyright © Sharon Canfield Dorsey
November 2025.
All rights reserved.
ISBN:
Published by High Tide Publications, Inc.
www.Hightidepublications.com
Deltaville, Virginia

Thank you for choosing this authorized edition of *Been There, Done that...Happy Dance*. At High Tide, our mission is to discover, promote, and publish the work of talented authors over 50. Your support by purchasing an authorized copy is crucial in helping us bring their work to you.

Respecting copyright law by refraining from reproducing or scanning any part without our permission is not just about obeying the law, but also about respecting the authors' rights and enabling us to continue supporting them. Your decision to purchase an authorized edition is not only a personal choice, but a valuable contribution to the authors and the entire publishing process. It allows us to bring their work to you and to a wider community of readers.

Your support in our mission to bring the work of our authors to a wider audience is deeply appreciated. Thank you for choosing to purchase an authorized edition.

Book design by Firebellied Frog Graphic Design

Cover Design: Vivien Mann

Visit the author's website at www. sharoncanfielddorsey.com.

Dedication

I dedicate this book to the two people who made my thirteen published books possible- *Vivien Mann* and *Jeanne Johansen.*

Vivien is a talented artist who illustrated two of my children's books, *Herman, the Hermit Crab,* and *Revolt of the Teacups.* She is also the creator of the unique paintings that became covers for most of my other books. She is my forever friend who encourages my writing, listens to me, who loves and supports my whole family. Besides her paintings, jewelry, and artwork in mixed mediums, she is a dedicated social worker who makes the world a better place every day.

Jeanne is the incredibly inspired and creative publisher who makes my books come to life in amazing ways. Her company, High Tide Publications, Inc., is dedicated to the author over fifty. She is patient, wise, and a talented artist/writer in her own right.

My books are beautiful and unique due to Jeanne's painstaking care with each one. Through the years we've worked together, she has become my dear friend. I will be forever grateful she came into my life.

Table of Contents

Dedication
1 - Let's Go Back in Time
    Time Travel with Me…Back to 1950   1
    A Woman's Place   2
    To Grandmother's House We Go   3
    My First Christmas Shopping Adventure   6
    The Christmas Box   8
    Changing Seasons   10
    If We Could Turn Back Time 100 Years…   12

2 - Family Ties
    Behind the Mask   15
    My Dad's Story   17
    Power to the Matriarchy   19
    Country Girl Goes to the City   20
    Prayers of a Single Mom   23
    Going Home Again   24
    Home   25
    Sharon and Don's Incredibly Happy Wedding   26
    Grandchildren and Teacups   28
    Grandchildren Rock   29
    Bookworms, Real and Imaginary   30
    Fifty Years Wise, Darling Daughter, Shannon   32
    Changing Traditions   34
    Time Flies   36

3 - Small Towns Rock
    Country Living, Fun And Folly   41
    The Run For The Wall   43
    Valentine Winners And Losers   44
    A Small-Town 4th Of July, Parades And Prisoners   46
    Patriotism Lives   48
    On The Way To The Greatest State Fair On Earth   50
    Summertime On The River   54
    Ghost And Goblins   56

4 - Travel with Me

Paradise Found	61
Westward Ho! Sights And Sounds Of The Southwest	64
The Elephants Who Came To Dinner	67
Strange Things I Know About America	69
Well-Behaved Women Rarely Make History	71
Scenes From The Vatican, April 26, 2025	75
My Fantasy Life	77

5 - Life Lessons

All I Need To Know, I Learned From The Easter Bunny	81
Letter To My Ten-Year-Old Self	82
Things Every Woman Should Have And Know Today	83
Spring Cleaning – Closet Closure	85
Like Sand Through An Hour-Glass	87
As We Remember	88
The Circle Of Life	89
Forever Friendships	90
A Writing Life	93
I Used To Think…	95

6 - The "O" Word

Older Than Dirt	99
Body Betrayal	102
When is OLD?	104
Aging with Friends	106
Embracing Oldness	107
Oh, Those Birthdays!	110
The Soundtrack Of My Life	111
My Love/Hate Relationship With Aging	112
Downsizing Can Bring You Joy	113
Eighty-Two…Who Knew?	114

7 - My Soap Box

Technology And Me	117
Computer Warfare	118
Teachers Deserve More Money And More Respect!!!!	119
Indigenous Peoples' Day	121
The World Needs A Talking Stick	123
Acceptance can Make our World a Better Place	124
Gay Pride	126
Colors of our Lives	129
We, the People	131

The Rescuers	132
Woman, the Change Maker	133
The Other Ten Commandments	134

8 - Journey to the Pandemic

Journey To The Pandemic,	137
A Day At A Time, Feb. 20, 2019-Feb. 20, 2020	137

9 - When the World Shut Down

History Repeats Itself	173
A Very Scary Fairy Tale	175
Grocery Shopping in the Age Of Covid-19	176
Six Feet Apart	178
Scenes from the Battlefield…	179
Remember When…	180
Food Is Love	181
Time-Like A Picnic	183
Around And Around We Go	184
America's Grand Reopening - What Happens Next??	185
Our New World	187
Spring's Glorious Entrance (3-Stanza Tanka)	189

10 - Always Leave 'Em Laughin'

I Often Wonder	193
The Summertime Open-Toed Shoe Pledge	194
Shoe Shock	195
Why God Made Mothers	196
(As explained by third graders.)	196
The Gifts Real Moms Would Like For Mother's Day	197
Mom's Revenge	198
Lively Limericks	199
Merry Haiku Christmas	200
A Change In Christmas Plans	201
'Twas The Week After Christmas	203
I Used To…	204

About the Author

Other Books by Sharon Canfield Dorsey

Let's Go Back in Time

Part 1

Been There - Done That
Happy Dance!

Time Travel with Me ...Back to 1950

I was seven.

A stamp was 7 cents.

Hair-cuts were 30 cents.

Gas was 25 cents a gallon.

Hotels charged $2 a night.

Harry S. Truman was president.

The minimum wage was under $1.

A one-day stay in the hospital was $15.

All About Eve won the Academy award.

The electric typewriter had just been invented.

The highest paid baseball players earned $50,000 a year.

Few people believed fast food restaurants would catch on.

Parents forbid their teenagers to listen to that evil rock 'n roll.

Married women who worked outside the home were soundly criticized.

Elvis Presley's gyrating on the Ed Sullivan Show was declared scandalous.

People worried the new Volkswagen would open the door to too many foreign businesses.

A Woman's Place

In 1955, an anonymous article, called the *Good Wife's Guide*, was published in several women's magazines. I became aware of it when I was cleaning out my mother's house after her passing, and found it in a stack of old papers. The fact that she kept it says a lot about the female mindset of that time and what they believed was expected of them. *The Guide* inspired this poem. The first phrase of each stanza is from 1955. The second is my 2025 rebuttal.

In the 1950's	In 2025
Have a delicious meal ready when your husband comes home from work.	Show me a man who can cook, and I'll run away with him tomorrow.
Dress, do your hair, and take fifteen minutes to rest before he arrives home. You must look your best.	I happen to like my sweats, and the dog ate my hair brush.
Try to be interesting for him. It is your wifely duty.	Steven bit the new neighbor kid, and Shannon threw up in your shoes.
The house should be immaculate when he arrives, with a drink waiting.	Are you home already? I've been binge-watching *The Crown*.
Teach your children to be obedient and silent when their father is home.	Kids! You promised me you would not slime your father!
Listen to him, for his topics of conversation are more important than yours.	Sue from **Book Club** says your friend, Joe, is sleeping with the baby-sitter.
Don't complain if he comes home late or stays out all night because he is the master of the house, and you have no right to question.	No, you can't come in, and yes, I did have the locks changed. Your clothes are at Goodwill and your motorcycle is in the pool.

To Grandmother's House We Go

As an adult, I was fortunate to be able to travel to beautiful places, strange places, exotic places. As a child, I only traveled to one place-my grandparents' house, each summer in August, for two wonderful weeks. They lived in Point Pleasant, West Virginia, which was about a five-hour drive from our home. August heat and no auto air-conditioning dictated early morning departure, usually 5 a.m. Three sleepy kids packed in with suitcases, snacks, toys-you get the picture. It didn't help that at least one of us, usually me, got car sick.

After hours in the car, we would get excited as we turned off the main highway onto the dirt road that led to the house. Grandma liked to grumble affectionately to Grandaddy about the God-forsaken location, so far from town, shopping, and all the things she liked to do. She never let him forget that retiring to the country was his idea.

When we approached the fish ponds, my brothers and I would get rowdy because we knew we were getting close. Grandaddy took us fishing there in the evenings. Grandma went along, collecting cattails for her flower arrangements. Masses of tangled rose bushes and blackberry brambles tumbled into the road, narrowing the passage. Each summer, we'd pick buckets of blackberries for Grandma to can and freeze, or make into delicious cobblers that we'd devour with homemade ice cream on steamy August nights.

Grandaddy always carried home armfuls of the pink, sweet-smelling wild roses because they were Grandma's favorites. She would declare this years' crop of roses, "the best ever!" and stuff them into crystal vases in every room of their sturdy cinder-block house. They built the house themselves, with the help of friends and relatives, then furnished it with all the things they had collected in their travels during Grandaddy's working years as a saw-filer with a large construction company.

Grandma loved souvenirs and what-nots, dustibles, my children call them now. At Grandma's house, they perched on every table and window sill, atop starched, crocheted doilies she turned out by the dozens. I don't think I ever saw my grandmother sitting down without some kind of needlework in her hands. She taught me to crochet and embroider. During our summer visits, she helped me to create pillowcases and scarves for my hope chest, that collection of household things young ladies of the 40's and 50's were expected to stockpile for their wedding day. Grandma said when Grandaddy proposed, her own hope chest was full of wonderful things that she could proudly contribute to their first home together. I still have some of those first crude doilies we crafted together. I thought they were beautiful because she told me they were.

Grandma also gave me my first cooking lessons during those summer visits. We concentrated on the important foods like lemon pie and pineapple upside-down cake. We created salads too, macaroni and potato salads, and deviled eggs. I was allowed to mash the boiled egg-yokes and mix in the mayonnaise and mustard with a touch of vinegar for that just right tart flavor. It was a proud day when Grandma decided I was old enough to chop the homemade pickles for the salads.

Frying the chicken was a different matter. Grandma always did that herself, dredging the chicken pieces in a pie pan filled with flour and secret seasonings that make her fried chicken renowned at all the family picnics. I never graduated to fried chicken, but I was allowed to mash the potatoes for Sunday dinner while Grandma made the gravy from the chicken scrapings in the big iron skillet. We would wear aprons that she had embroidered for us, mine hanging to my ankles, and grin at each other over our cooking pots. Even now, when I eat lemon pie or fried chicken, I remember and miss her.

As we rounded the last curve of the dusty road and headed up the hill, we'd forget about the long hours in the hot, cramped car.

We knew Grandma would be sitting in the swing on the screened porch overlooking the driveway, fanning herself and watching for us, as excited as we were. She was always in her apron because she'd been up since dawn, baking cakes, pies and ham, and making salads and homemade bread. Oh, and fudge. She knew we loved her chocolate and peanut butter fudge, full of walnuts from Grandaddy's trees. She'd rip the apron off when she saw us round the curve and hobble down the steps to meet us. Grandma had been crippled all her life from a childhood fall. But she never considered herself handicapped. She managed to do everything that everybody else did.

Grandaddy would be in the apple orchard or in the yard, setting up the croquet set. He was the family croquet and horseshoes champion. He loved having new victims to beat. He never let us win, just because we were children. When we did occasionally win a game, it was an occasion to celebrate.

If we came to visit in late summer, Grandaddy might be tending his fire-pit. He'd dig a hole in the ground, and we'd roast ears of corn from his garden. We learned not to pig out completely on the fresh, sweet corn, because there would be watermelon later. He carried the melons from the field in early morning and put them in the root cellar where it was cool. They were sweet and juicy on hot summer evenings.

He would come running too, from wherever he was, his old straw hat in one hand, his snuff box in the other. Grandma grumbled about his snuff dipping but I noticed when we went into town for groceries, she always brought him a new can. He'd grin and kiss her on the cheek. She's blush like a young girl and say, "You old devil!" Grandaddy was living with my mother when he died at age 94 (we had lost Grandma ten years before), and he still enjoyed his snuff when she wasn't watching.

I've stayed in beautiful hotels with every amenity and slept under the stars in the shadow of Anasazi ruins, but nothing ever quite matched the cozy magic of my bedroom under the eaves of Grandma and Grandaddy's house, with its feather bed and sheets that smelled like lavender.

My First Christmas Shopping Adventure

I woke up at seven and peeped out the frosty window. No snow, no sleet, just a hint of sunshine. We could go Christmas shopping today! Mom and Daddy had promised this would be the year I could do my own Christmas shopping for our family of four. It was an exciting adventure for a girl of eight in 1951.

I wolfed down my breakfast of fried eggs, sausage, and biscuits without the usual savoring of strawberry preserves on the last half of the biscuit. Today there were more important things to do. I paced while everyone got dressed and Daddy warmed up the car. There was no snow, but it was 30 degrees outside with frost on the windows.

Finally, we all piled into the car—Mom, Daddy, younger brother, Homer, and drove the eight miles to the nearby town of Rainelle. Daddy found a choice parking spot in front of **Murphy's Five and Dime** and we went inside. "Frosty the Snowman" was playing on the sound system and the store was a fairyland, aglow with lights and tinsel. Daddy handed me a $5 bill. I folded it carefully, put it in my plastic coin purse, and stowed the purse in my coat pocket, buttoning it to be sure that precious money would not fall out. Daddy wandered off to **Hunting Supplies**; Mom, with Homer in tow, to **Housewares**, and I was on my own.

I had planned my strategy ahead of time. I could spend $1.50 on each person and have fifty cents left for a bag of penny candy. I decided to start with Mom's gift. There were so many pretty things…bottles of perfume, packaged in see-through crinkly paper, tied with red and green ribbons… white handkerchiefs embroidered with pink and blue flowers, displayed under cellophane in square gift boxes…tiny gold angels on sparkling chains, fastened securely into black velvet boxes…so many choices. I settled on the gold angel necklace. I looked around to be sure Mom wasn't nearby before handing my five-dollar bill to the smiling cashier. The surprise was everything.

Shopping for Daddy was easier. I debated between a package of warm socks, a red cigarette lighter, or a tiny silver pocket knife. The pocket knife won.

When I was sure Mom and Homer were still nowhere in sight, I tackled my last shopping challenge, my four-year-old brother. There were two long aisles of toys-red fire trucks, Tinker Toys, wind-up dogs that barked and waddled across the floor, cowboy guns with holsters. I agonized but finally decided on a Gene Autry gun and holster.

When I counted my change after all my purchases, I had twenty-eight cents left. Homer and I carefully selected our favorite candies, lingering over Coconut Slices, Taffy, Candy Cigarettes, Pops, Fruit Chews, and Dubble Bubble Gum. With our brown paper bags clutched tightly, we grinned at each other and declared it a good day.

On Christmas morning, Daddy said the silver knife was exactly what he needed to carry in his pocket when he went to work every day in the coal mines. Homer immediately strapped on the Gene Autry gun and holster and screamed when Mom wouldn't let him wear it to bed. Mom loved the gold angel necklace. She wore it to church and on special occasions. When friends admired it, she always proudly explained, "Sharon gave it to me for Christmas."

When my brother and I cleaned out our childhood home after our mother's death at age eight-nine, we found, among the treasures she had saved all those years, the gold angel necklace, tarnished, but still safely ensconced in its faded velvet box.

The Christmas Box

My mother loved Christmas. She decorated everything in sight, and filled the house with the delicious, spicy aromas of ginger cookies, chocolate fudge, and rum-soaked fruitcake. She always hid our presents in her bedroom closet until December 25. We were allowed to open one gift on Christmas Eve. Everything else appeared magically on Christmas morning.

Mom would get so excited, she would wake us up if we didn't appear in the living room by 5 a.m. She still tortured us with that tradition when we were adults and returning home for the holidays. "Really, Mom?" we would whine, but we'd troop out, bleary-eyed to find her radiant in a beautiful dressing gown, giddy with excitement. By the time all the presents were opened, the room would be ankle-deep in paper. The noise level grew over the years as we added spouses and children to the crazy mix.

When the plundering of presents was over, a multi-course breakfast would appear, again, as if by magic. The Christmas meal was always served mid-afternoon. As I got older and understood how much work went into that preparation, I used to wonder how she did it all, standing over the stove, red-faced but still smiling. I realize now, Christmas Day was her gift to us, and it was her time to shine.

My Dad was a prankster. He loved playing jokes on people. Christmas was no exception. Each year, someone would receive a beautifully wrapped box containing coal or dirty bedroom slippers or sometimes, nothing. The year I was fourteen, it was my mother's turn to receive a gigantic, wrapped box, big enough to hide a person inside and too heavy to lift. We could tell she was almost afraid to open it. My Dad's gags had no boundaries. He was grinning, ear to ear. This was not a good sign.

We all helped tear the paper off. Dad used his pocket knife to cut open the carton. She began pulling out crumbled-up paper and smaller cardboard boxes, each one taped up and filled with things like rocks, marbles, sand. Yes, I did say sand. As she tore into box after box, Dad's grin got broader. Mom's face got redder as she hooted at each box. My little brothers were jumping up and down with the excitement of it all.

Finally, there was only one carton left in the bottom of the big box. She opened it to find…a smaller box…an even smaller box…and finally, a tiny box. Inside the tiny box was a blue velvet ring box. Inside that was the most beautiful diamond ring my young eyes had ever seen. My mother was speechless! Tears ran down her cheeks as Dad put the sparkling gift on her finger. I grabbed the Brownie camera and managed to capture the moment. I didn't know then, the back story of their courtship and secret elopement, but I noticed for the first time, the wedding ring she was wearing was worn thin. I would understand later, it was worn from all the years of hard work those hands had performed for all of us.

I never thought of my Dad as romantic, but that Christmas, he managed to pull off the most romantic gift ever!

Changing Seasons

Do you have a favorite season of the year? My feelings about each season can be traced all the way back to my 50's childhood.

Growing up, spring meant a flurry of activity. As winter's ice and snow dissolved into sunny days, my mother, the master cleaner, recruited my younger brothers and me to help her turn our small house upside down. Patchwork quilts were spread on clotheslines; curtains were taken down and washed; rugs were carried out to the sidewalk and scrubbed; walls were washed down, and baseboards painted. Nothing escaped my mother's scrutiny. While she was purifying our space, my dad was plowing and planting our summer garden. We, kids, were also expected to pitch in, dropping corn kernels in long, even rows and covering the seed potatoes with rich, damp earth.

Summertime signaled no school, so there was lots of time for softball in the yard with cousins, marble tournaments in the dirt; picnic lunches of bologna/mayo sandwiches with Kool-Aide, under the trees, and bare feet. On Sundays, we'd visit aunts and uncles who lived nearby or drive out to one of the state parks for a real picnic, complete with Mom's fried chicken, macaroni salad, and deviled eggs. In July or August, we'd make the five-hour drive to visit our grandparents for a glorious week of badminton, horseshoes, corn roasts, and homemade ice cream. If the coal miners were given time off for the 4th of July holiday, we'd go camping.

Fall covers the West Virginia hills with scarlet and gold splendor. For us, that signaled last minute chores-digging the potatoes, filling the cellar with apples, pears; canning the last of the green beans; making blackberry jam; filling the large ceramic pickling jar with ears of corn. It was also the time when the Sears, Roebuck and Montgomery Ward catalogues arrived. Nighttime hours were spent on the important task of choosing new school clothes for all of us. Money was always scarce, so Mom made it very clear that our choices were limited to the lowest price range. But, still, it was exciting when the huge box arrived and we could try on our bounty. School was my favorite place, so fall was one of those seasons I most looked forward to.

Winter is probably my least favorite time of the year as an adult. The stark, bare trees, gray skies, and short days seem to darken my spirits. As a child, however, it was a fun time of sleigh-riding, building snowmen, clumping to the bus stop in waist high snow. No, school didn't stop for a little, or a lot, of that white stuff. For my mom, winter was a time of rest from summer's gardening, gathering, and preserving chores. She and my aunts would gather after we left for school to gossip and work on quilting/sewing projects. Wish I could have heard the stories told around those quilting frames.

As we face the effects of climate change, seasonal habits have changed too. We now have to worry more about hurricanes, tornados, fires, and massive snowstorms. Carefree summers and peaceful winters seem a faraway fantasy, frozen in time.

IF WE COULD TURN BACK TIME 100 YEARS...

We would be moving at a much slower pace.
Speed limit was ten miles per hour.

We could buy gas and drugs at the same time.
Fuel for cars was only sold in drug stores,
along with marijuana, heroin, and morphine.
The average worker earned $200 a year.

We would be communicating via letter.
Only 8% of people had a telephone.
Your doctor probably had no college education.
He learned through on-the-job training.

BUT...

There would be more trees than parking lots.
The passenger pigeon would not be extinct.
Our daily food might not be poisoning us.
Hurricanes, tornadoes, wildfires would be a rarity.

If we could continue progress, but correct our mistakes,
maybe our air would be clear, our water clean.
Perhaps we would look up at the stars more,
appreciate and protect the blessings of our planet.

If we could turn back time and do better,
maybe Mother Nature would not be crying.

Family Ties

Part 2

Been There - Done That
Happy Dance!

Behind the Mask

When I look in the mirror these days, I see the face of my mother. I often find myself repeating her words, and worse, now understanding why she said them. Becoming one's mother is not an uncommon complaint. You can even buy buttons and t-shirts proclaiming this alarming metamorphous. I find myself feeling even closer to my mother since writing my memoir and examining so much of her life.

I do, however, question whether I could have lived the life she lived without becoming beaten down by it. Raising three children in a two-bedroom house without running water or indoor plumbing, heated by a pot-bellied coal stove, could not have been easy. Her red, cracked hands were testimony to washings hung out in freezing weather; harvests reaped from hand-hoed fields; and no money for luxuries like fragranced hand creams.

When I look back one more generation, I marvel even more at the strength and tenacity of my grandmothers, who grew up, married, and reared their own children in even worse circumstances in the coal fields of Appalachia. One of them spent the early years of her marriage living in a tent home, built with a wooden floor, canvas walls and roof. Could I have done that? I guess we grow into whatever challenges we face.

If I journey two generations deeper behind the mask that is me, I find a face with high cheekbones, dark, straight hair and inscrutable staring eyes. My aunts used to tell me they thought I looked like her. But they couldn't tell me much more about my Cherokee great grandmother. She is listed on the Cherokee tribal rolls. Her family migrated from North Carolina to West Virginia. But we don't know how or when. Did they escape the infamous Trail of Tears?

Between four and eight thousand Cherokee died on that march. Was my great-grandmother one of the lucky survivors? She would have been about ten at the beginning of that relocation of sixteen-thousand Indians from North Carolina to Oklahoma. Could I have survived that march?

When I look into the mirror that doesn't lie, I see a mother, daughter, sister, friend, child of the universe. Behind the aging mask that is me, I see feathered braids, calloused hands of pioneer farmers, bent bodies of coal miners-all keepin' on, keepin' on, to build a country and culture that provided a better life for me than they could have imagined.

My Dad's Story

My father, Carl Eartman Canfield, was the first married man drafted in his small Appalachian Mountains town of Charmco, West Virginia, during World War II. My parents had no savings. My mother tells me we lived in a renovated chicken house while he was away. I was six months old.

Dad was stationed at a Naval base in the Great Lakes. One freezing winter night, his guard duty relief didn't show up. His feet and legs were badly damaged from the long hours in the cold. He suffered severe pain the rest of his life.

Despite that, he returned home after his discharge to his job in the mines, digging coal on his knees for twelve hours every night. He had no car, so he walked or hitch-hiked the six miles to the mines and back.

When he was able to buy a small home, he spent his off-hours in his garden. Tilling the soil, hunting and fishing were his favorite things to do, so we were never hungry. He shared the garden abundance with neighbors, leaving baskets on their porches.

The hard work, the constant pain could have turned my dad into a bitter, angry man. It did make him drink too much, but he never lost his sense of humor or his love of jokes. Pity the naïve friend who fell victim to his pranks. That person might find a snake skin curled up on his pillow or a whoopee cushion on his truck seat.

Dad loved his country, was an avid politician, a proud Democrat, campaigning and driving seniors to the polls. His connections helped me get my first job interview for a secretarial job in the office of the governor of West Virginia.

My dad's life was difficult but he never gave up on his responsibilities to support his family; on his commitment to helping his friends, neighbors; on his loyalty to his state and his country; or on his cock-eyed optimist's approach to life.

Dad died in his sixties of complications from black lung disease, that evil enemy of West Virginia's underground warriors, after relentlessly battling the powers that be for disability benefits from those years in the mines. He won that battle, but sadly, lost his own.

Thankfully, his long, determined fight would provide income and medical benefits for my mother for the rest of her life. It gave him great satisfaction to know he could still take care of her after he was gone. His name is engraved on a Miner's Memorial near the mouth of the mine where he worked for so many years.

Power to the Matriarchy

My red-haired mother, Macil June Kuhl Canfield, was a tough broad, an independent spirit, despite being a housewife in the 40's, 50's, and 60's, and despite having no money of her own. She raised three children in a two-bedroom frame house in Appalachia with no indoor bathroom or running water, heated by a pot-bellied stove, the wife of a coal miner who drank too much.

My brothers and I were grown when our father died of black lung, after years of abusive labors in the depths of the mines. My mother grieved, then reinvented herself. At age fifty-one, she created a resume and to our great surprise, was quickly hired as a Temp Aide to the West Virginia Legislature. Her fiery red hair and matching sense of humor caught the eye of a widowed accountant/legislator, ten years her senior, who swept her off her feet. He loved to travel. She had always wanted to see the country. It was a match meant to be.

They were happy wanderers/companions for many years. When he became ill and bedfast, she cared for him at home, as she had my dad, refusing to leave his side until he passed, more than two years later.

Again, she grieved and we wondered if her sparkle and zest for living were gone forever.

We should have known better than to worry. She picked herself up and went on with her life, visiting children and grand-children, enjoying lunches out and shopping with Red Hat friends.

When she left us at eighty-nine, she was still berating us for taking away her car keys.

Country Girl Goes to the City

Once upon a time, a coal miner's daughter from the West Virginia hills moved to the swankiest neighborhood in the Sacramento Valley of California, to live with a wealthy aunt and uncle and attend college at American River Junior College.

The first part of the adventure was the Cadillac road trip across the country with Aunt Dorothy and Uncle Claude, who quickly became Unc and Aunt D. This country girl had never stayed in a hotel or eaten in a real restaurant. Dairy Queen was the only eating establishment in our little town of Charmco, where we ordered hot dogs through the drive-thru on very special occasions.

When we arrived at the gated community that would be my home for the next year, I was speechless. The huge ranch-style home, at the end of a tree-lined lane, looked like something out of the movies to me. The pool and artfully landscaped patio in the back completed the scene. My room was beautiful and overlooked the pool. MY room! I had shared a room with an eight-years-younger brother for years. Having my own room, any room, was a dream come true.

The next day, Unc drove me to the community college and helped me register for classes. It would be our routine for the next eleven months. He would drop me off in the morning and pick me up in the afternoon. On the way home, we would chatter about our days. He was a very busy real estate mogul. I didn't realize until much later in life, how many business trips he had to cancel in order to be my chauffeur. Aunt D was an elementary school principal whose day often extended way beyond my 9-4 school day, so Unc was the one who made the sacrifices.

Unc was my Dad's youngest brother of a family of seven siblings. Their mother, my grandmother, was struck and killed by a car in her thirties, so the kids basically raised themselves. Dad left school in the eighth grade to get a job in the coal mines to help support the family. One by one, three other brothers did the same. The two young sisters took over housekeeping chores. They were all determined that at least one of them should get an education. Unc was the youngest, so he was the logical choice. He graduated from high school, joined the Marines, and used his VA benefits to go to college. He fell in love with California, and Aunt D, and they decided to make California their home.

Every summer, they drove home to visit the family. Their plan to take me home with them to California the summer I graduated from high school was hatched with my parents without any consultation with me. I had a serious boyfriend and had planned to go to college close to home. I had applied for and received a National Defense Student Loan because of outstanding grades, but my parents would not let me accept it. They had two goals-get me away from the boyfriend, and get me into a college that was free. Junior college in California at that time was free to everyone. So, kicking and screaming, my California adventure began.

Unc and Aunt D were unable to have children of their own. They welcomed me with open arms, but didn't quite know what to do with a teenager they barely knew. I taught them that pizza and hot dogs were just as delicious as steak and vegetables, though, maybe not as healthy. They taught me to manage my time and helped me develop good study habits. I also taught them to loosen up and have more fun. My new school friends became regular visitors to the pool and the big house rang with laughter.

Unc had managed to purchase huge amounts of property in the Sacramento Valley when it was just a farming and ranching area and acreage was cheap. That acreage became subdivisions and shopping centers and Unc became rich. He also became skilled at investments and his portfolio grew. When he died a few years ago, he was a billionaire. He built his fortune with frugality and vision. He would talk to me about all those things in our afternoons after school. He instilled in me a sense of openness to opportunity; a belief that anything is possible; an appreciation of education; an awareness of the importance of travel to widen our view of the world. By the time I went back to West Virginia at the end of that year, I felt ready to tackle whatever the universe sent my way.

Unc also set out to tackle a new challenge at the end of that year. He enrolled in chiropractic school in Iowa, embarking on a new career at the age of forty-five. He graduated, went back to California, and practiced for twenty years, often providing care for those who needed it, but couldn't afford to pay. When he retired for the second time, he and Aunt D moved back to WV to live among his siblings, nieces and nephews, his circle complete.

Prayers of a Single Mom

Help me sit through the Star Wars Trilogy one more time with my nine-year-old son, without becoming paranoid.

Slip me some reassuring answers at bedtime, when my little girl, smelling of bubble bath and bubble gum, asks, "When is Daddy coming home?"

Give me a sense of humor for those days when the car won't start, or the cat gets stuck on the roof and forgets how to get down.

Give me enough mechanical know-how to see through the unscrupulous mechanic, who tells me I need a new transmission, when all I really need is a tune-up.

Teach me, quickly, how to whittle a miniature car from a block of wood, in time for next week's Pinewood Derby.

Teach me to see the positive, rather than the negative in my new household chores.

Help me to enjoy house painting and grass mowing, when I'd rather be baking cookies.

Transform me into a financial genius, who can stretch four weeks pay, through five long weeks.

Give me a reserve of energy at the end of my working day, to begin my other working day at home.

Endow me with forgiveness for the husband and father who deserted us.

Replace the anger and sadness with hope.

Help me rear my children to be loving, responsible adults, who feel confident and good about themselves.

Give me the courage to trust again. And, if you can possibly manage it, send someone kind and loving to share our lives.

Going Home Again

I used to live in the cream-colored house on the corner,
the one with the Williamsburg Blue shutters and door.
The rickety fence still leans, evidence of daily abuse
by multitudes of boisterous, climbing children.

The Charlie Brown sapling I planted is resplendent in autumn rust,
now proudly full grown, like my two kids, who put down roots in
that house, then ripped them up to go in search of
enlightenment, adventure, and themselves.

The house wears its twenty-five years of birthday parties,
graduations, and Christmases more lightly than I.
Those seasons that slipped away so quickly, now
resonate in every inch of my heart, bones, and mind.

The memories of laughter, tears, conflict, and peace,
flash through, leaving a melancholy residue of faintly
echoing voices, leaving me feeling as if I, too,
might need a fresh coat of Williamsburg Blue paint.

Home

What is home?
Is it a place, a memory, or is it a person who makes us feel safe, loved?

Where is home?
Is it our birthplace, where we grew up, where we still return?

My brothers and I always referred to our hometown as home,
but our actual childhood home no longer exists.

Recently, I drove past the house where I raised my children.
It wears its twenty-five years of growing-up chaos well.

There's no evidence of the birthday party sleep-overs,
the Star Wars popcorn nights, the heart-broken teenage tears.

When I moved from their childhood home, I wondered if my children would be sad. Their response answers the first question.

"Home will always be where you are."

Sharon and Don's Incredibly Happy Wedding

It was a rainy, dreary Tuesday, April 8, 2008. "Let's get married," Don said.

"Yes, let's!" Sharon agreed and suddenly, the sun was shining through the rain.

We searched our closets for something red to wear, because it was, indeed, a Red-Letter Day, a great way, we decided, to celebrate our twenty years of togetherness. Off to the courthouse we went, in search of a license. Alas, no senior discount, despite Don's charm. "Full price," demanded the clerk, whose sunny smile hadn't yet reached her face.

Next, Don called son, Steven, in Kentucky, to ask for the bride's hand, to which son replied, "It's about time." He offered to spring for a reception at Hardees. Don, my hero, insisted on an upgrade to Burger King.

Daughter, Shannon, upon receiving the glad tidings, wanted to leave work immediately and help with the plans. I think she was afraid we'd change our minds. But we were steadfast in our determination to tie the knot.

In between a doctor appointment, Mary Kay deliveries, and a fast run through the grocery store, we spread the shock and awe among our friends, instructing them to show up at 7:30, wearing red. We decided the guests would dine on our favorite foods-cheesecake (mine), peanut butter sandwiches (Don's), and sparkling cider.

Steven sent spring flowers, which arrived just in time. Shannon decorated the table with another lovely bouquet. Don gallantly presented red roses to the bride. Our still-amazed friends arrived early, arms full of food and gifts. I think someone leaked the word that we planned to feed them cheesecake and peanut butter sandwiches.

At 7:30, we all gathered in our living room, with Don resplendent in his bear claw bedroom slippers, our friends wearing red and sporting broad smiles. Since this was before the everyday magic of Zoom, Shannon held the phone up so Steven could listen, because he had demanded proof of this earth-shattering event.

Marriage Commissioner Gilley, looking dapper in a red tie, did a beautiful reading about marriage which brought tears. He said, "Do you...?"

We said, "I do."

He said, "I now pronounce..."

We kissed. Everybody cried and hugged everybody else.

Then we laughed and ate until all the food was gone, including all the peanut butter sandwiches.

GRANDCHILDREN AND TEACUPS

I am a doting grandmother to Adaline, Emma and Zachary. I am constantly entertained by their sense of fun, their talents, their intelligence and their kind, loving hearts. Zachary, the youngest, is the happiest when he's playing with cars, trucks and construction equipment, anything that *vrooms*! Adaline and Emma love dressing up their Barbie's and their American Girl dolls. But they are also talented little artists, spending hours drawing everything from self-portraits to teacups with faces and personalities. Their teacup pictures were the inspiration for my children's book, ***Revolt of the Teacups***.

I wrote the story around the tea cup characters they had drawn. My talented artist/friend, Vivien Mann, brought the characters and book to life with her wonderful illustrations. Adaline and Emma were excited to get cover credit as Illustrators in Training. When they came to visit at Christmastime, we debuted the book and they autographed copies for family and friends. I thought my heart was going to pop out of my chest with pride in our finished product. It's a day I will always remember. I hope they will too.

Grandchildren Rock

They dance and they giggle,
give out lots of hugs.

They're wide-eyed at rainbows.
They even like bugs.

They're loving and trusting.
They're smarter than us.

If something's not perfect,
they shrug, "What's the fuss?"

They remind us of wonderful
years that are past,

when their parents were children.
The time went so fast.

Bookworms, Real and Imaginary

I've been asked where I get my ideas for my children's books. They surface from strange places.

One February, I received an unusual birthday gift from a friend-a fluffy yellow bookworm with big, googly eyes. My friend said, "I think this should be the character for your next children's book." He WAS adorable but what was his story?

I did some research and learned that the scientific name for bookworms is *Anobium Punctatum. An-o-bi-um Punct-a-tum*! I liked the sound of it but would a five-year-old think it was a fun name? Baby bookworms eat the pulpy paper in books, then morph into wood beetles who drill holes in trees and furniture. How could that cute, yellow creature with the big eyes destroy books??? Ah, ha! I had my story. My bookworm would want to read the books, not eat them. My fingers couldn't fly across the keys fast enough. Buddy and Ballerina would be the main characters, and they would save the library books.

When I sent the finished story off to Jeanne Johansen, my publisher at High Tide Publications, she said it was, "supercalifragilisticexpialidocious." She also had a great idea, "Let's ask your granddaughters, (Adaline, age 10 and Emma, age 7) to illustrate it." The girls' teacup drawings had been the inspiration for my second children's book, *Revolt of the Teacups* and they were listed on the back cover as "Illustrators in Training." Why not give them full rein and see what happens? So that's what we did. The result was amazing. Buddy and Ballerina debuted in time for Christmas, 2018. What fun!

My first children's book, *Herman the Hermit Crab and the Mystery of the Big, Black Shiny Thing* also evolved from an interesting story. My husband, Don, and I liked to vacation on a tiny island in the British Virgin Islands, called Cooper Island. The resort consisted of six small cottages, an open-air restaurant, some wild goats, and the most beautiful clear, blue water we'd ever seen.

One morning, an oil bottle washed up on the beach. We carried it back to the cottage and left it by the steps for maintenance to pick up. When we left the cottage that night to walk to dinner, the black bottle was surrounded by hermit crabs, dragging their shell houses to form a circle around the mysterious thing. The next morning, they were still there, worshipping at the shrine of the oil bottle. I wrote the story of Herman and his hermit crab friends that day as a surprise for my grandchildren, hoping someday it would become a book. My talented artist/friend, Vivien, flew to Virginia from Arizona and together, we crafted *Herman the Hermit Crab and the Mystery of the Big, Black Shiny Thing*. Holding that first published book in my hands was a dream come true.

Fifty Years Wise, Darling Daughter, Shannon

Birthdays, like birthday cards, come in a variety pack.

Your first birthday was spent with Dad, me, Mimi, and doting big brother, Steven, who fed you ice cream and opened your presents. He always looked after you, as you grew.

By two, you had mastered your own cake smearing and package ripping, but insisted on sharing all the presents with that brother, the beginning of your generous, kind heart.

As you grew, so did the celebrations-everything from Pin the Head on the Skeleton, to painting pumpkins, to painting teenage faces. Halloween and birthdays were synonymous.

As an adult, that kind heart provided a safe-haven for furry friends-from ducks in the bathtub, to sock-snatching ferrets, rabbits, and multitudes of much-loved dogs and cats.

Adulting was not always easy. You refused to let divorce bring you down. You earned your Bachelors and Masters degrees with honors, while holding down a stressful fulltime job.

Just when life with your loving, supportive spouse, A. J., was great and you felt justified in wearing that "Life is Good" sweatshirt, BOOM! I decided to downsize and move!

You were there with love and a strong back for all of it-boxes packed, carloads carried away, hundreds of trips up and down stairs, plus reminding me to rest and eat.

You have grown into a strong, smart, compassionate woman, beautiful inside and out. I am incredibly proud to be your mom and your friend. Fifty is a freeing number.

It's just the beginning of more satisfying, fun, years to come.

Changing Traditions

Christmas is a time of traditions that we hold tightly…the much-loved decorations we put on the tree every year…Grandma's recipes we faithfully reproduce…the rituals on Christmas Eve and Christmas morning. But as our children grow up and grow into families of their own, it's not always possible to maintain those traditions. We must embrace the changes, just as our parents had to do, and remember that being together is all that matters-whether it's Christmas day, the day after, or a week later.

Belated Christmas

They tumble out of my house the same way they tumbled in-
sippy cup and mugs in hand, mini I-Pads under their arms,
giggles echoing in the quiet, frosty after-Christmas morning.

Adaline, the ten-year-old, big-sisters the little ones into their car seats.
Emma, the bright-eyed, six-year-old middle child,
tenderly tucks her new Cabbage Patch baby into the seat belt.

Zachary, the all-boy, five-year-old force of nature,
waves a battered Tigger, his irresitible, dimpled smile
displaying the space where his new front teeth will soon be.

Daughter-in-law, Amy, and son, Steven, circle the van,
tightening seat belts, squeezing in last minute snack bags,
fastening those ever-present I-Pads to the backs of seats.

They are like a well-oiled machine, packing every space,
carefully tucking newly-acquired Christmas presents
into their digitally-equipped Santa sleigh on wheels.

Their visit has been a whirlwind of presents, food, and laughter-
getting re-acquainted with grandchildren who are suddenly taller,
and squeezing in quiet catch-up talks by the fire after kids are in bed.

As I watch the firelight play on Steven and Amy's much-loved faces,
I silently lament the fact that they live out of daily hugging distance.
Kudos on these parents who could have stayed home by their own fire.

The kids wave as our Christmas visit comes to an end.
The Santa safari van moves on to the next grandparent visit.
Happiness is...all of us together...for three glorious days.

Time Flies

(Christmas, 2021)

Firelight flickers carve shadows on look-alike faces
as my son, Steven, and grandson, Zachary, bend over
a scrapbook, laughing at the images of a nine-year-old
boy who is now a graying adult and devoted father of three.

At Zachary's request to see photos of his dad at his
own age, scrapbooks were dutifully produced,
and we begin our slow walk down memory lane,
punctuated with giggles and more than one aha moment.

Zachary points out skinny legs, like his own, a mop of
recognizable dark hair, and front teeth still in need of braces.
He listens intently to stories of his dad's experiences as a
fifer in the Colonial Williamsburg Fife and Drum Corps.

Grand-daughters, Adaline and Emma, join the circle,
leaning over their dad's shoulder to see the photos of
birthday parties, Boy Scout outings, and ballgames in
the back yard. They listen as he identifies family members

who died before they were born and a grandfather they never
knew. A photo of a young Steven's girlfriend provokes more
giggles and brings up the subject of Adaline's first boyfriend,
along with a telling blush on her fourteen-year-old cheeks.

Zachary and Emma tease her mercilessly but it's obvious she's learned how to ignore them. I admire her newly-acquired composure. The transition from last year's little girl to this year's young woman leaves me with a lot to absorb.

A part of me wishes I could stop the clock and go back to those days when my own children were young and I could see them, hug them every day. Another part of me sees the future unfolding in front of me and is excited for the days that lie ahead.

Small Towns Rock

Part 3

Been There - Done That

Happy Dance!

Country Living, Fun And Folly

I grew up in the Appalachian Mountains of West Virginia. Our tiny home was nestled amidst several acres of forest. My dad cleared garden space and grew most of our food. When my husband and I bought a home, years later, #1 on the wish list was some land with trees. We found the perfect home on two wooded acres. We felt like pioneers, returning to our roots.

We staked out space for a vegetable garden and a flower bed. I began planting the roses I'd loved since childhood. I wanted a rose garden just like my grandmother Bessie tended. Some of my happiest memories were going out with her in early morning when the dew was still on the fragrant petals, picking the most perfect buds and filling crystal vases all over the house, even the bathroom. I couldn't wait to pick my own roses.

Nobody bothered to tell us a herd of twelve deer shared our wooded paradise. One morning, I discovered them happily munching on my prize roses, devouring the tender petals the way I devour my own guilty pleasure, pizza. They ignored my protests, carefully separating the petals from the briars. They ate 'til they were satisfied, then ambled on without even a thank you.

I thought, okay, they were here first. I guess I'll have to learn to share. They shared too, a doe hiding her newborn fawn under the forsythia bushes, while she ran off to forage briefly in the woods. I kept an eye on the baby until she returned, retrieved her offspring, and wandered away. I like to think she sensed I was a mother too, and knew her baby would be in good hands.

We also received no warning about the multitudes of acrobats disguised as squirrels, who flew from tree to tree and would in autumn, carry away every pear and apple on our trees, plus pillage the bird feeders. Unlike the doe, they gave us nothing in return for their thievery, unless you count the giggles their antics provoked every day.

There were other encounters with wildlife. There was the skunk who walked into the Have a Heart trap, set for a rabid fox, and would not budge 'til we lured him out with peanut butter, as we cowered behind a plastic tarp; the peacock who chased me into the house every time I tried to cut the wild daisies; and the huge white turkey who became so tame, he would fly up on the hood of our car when my husband was working on it and peer into the engine as if training to be a mechanic.

Our mulch pile was home to a couple of black snakes who liked to slither out and sun themselves on the black asphalt driveway. "They are controlling the mice and voles," I was told, so I agreed to let them stay, UNTIL the day I found one curled up on my white carpet in the living room. I still don't know who left a door open and let him in, but suffice to say, he was urged-no, forced-to find other surroundings.

Today I was sitting in my easy chair in front of the window, enjoying the warm sun streaming through, when I heard a strange pecking noise. Curiosity forced me outside where I discovered my neighbor's free range chickens, pecking away at the Styrofoam cover on my outdoor faucet. There was nothing left but the plastic fasteners. I think that qualifies as folly, don't you?

The Run for the Wall

They descend on my mountain hometown like swarms of noisy mosquitoes, five hundred strong, motorcycles of every size and noise decibel, bound for the Vietnam Memorial, in Washington, D. C.

Piloted by veterans of Vietnam, Iraq, Afghanistan, and every skirmish in between, they thunder down the mountain, into streets lined with families, coal miners, disabled vets in wheelchairs, all applauding, cheering, waving American flags.

For years, this coal mining town has welcomed **The Wall** vets who travel to D. C to honor their fallen comrades. They feed them, house them, honor their sacrifices. The hillside is covered with flags, representing the war casualties from the state.

An event that started with a small picnic, has become a town-wide celebration of remembrance. Vets look forward each year to this reunion with their West Virginia friends. This year, the mobile Vietnam Wall draws silent visitors and tears.

The Run for the Wall assures that those Americans who paid the ultimate price for our freedom, are remembered and revered.

Valentine Winners and Losers

Giggles and whispers echo around our small classroom. Red hearts decorate the blackboard, along with pink and white crepe paper streamers. We squirm, as all second graders do, on a long Friday afternoon, waiting impatiently for the Valentine's Day party to begin.

Teacher has promised to empty the paper-doilied, heart-covered valentine box at precisely 3:30 p.m. Two students stand by her desk, ready to deliver. This morning, we all placed our "Be mine!" and "You stole my heart," store-bought cards into the tissue box, now ruffled beyond recognition. It has been there all day, perched on the corner of Ms. Hedrick's desk, teasing us with the promise of fun to come.

The excitement builds…who will be the student who receives the most cards and is crowned valentine king or queen? The cards are distributed and we all look around to see who has the biggest pile. Everybody's stack looks about the same, so the counting begins. From the corner of my eye, I notice a friend, and then another, slip out of their seats and shyly place their cards on the teacher's desk. The murmur becomes a crescendo as we all rush to the front to add our cards to the growing pile, our grins wider than the mouth of the ruffled tissue box.

Ms. Hedrick is speechless, red-faced, and tearful as she accepts the bejeweled, gold-foil crown with all the dignity of a real queen. Back in our seats, the chatter subsiding, she stands, eyes bright, brushing gray hair back from her round face. Smiling broadly, she addresses her subjects. "I'm so very honored to be your queen. This is my best Valentine's Day ever!"

Every time I see a package of paper valentines, I briefly return to that day. Ms. Hedrick was what we called an old maid, in those days of unenlightenment. I think we made her day, maybe her year, by choosing her to be queen. We did a good thing. But I remember other years with mixed feelings. I was the valentine queen one year. I can't deny, it felt good to be the chosen one. There were other years, when we counted valentines, and I felt bad for my friends who didn't receive many. Thank goodness, schools no longer use Valentine's Day as a popularity contest.

A Small-Town 4th Of July...
Picnics, Parades, And Prisoners

My 4th of July memories are a mixture of camping trips, family picnics, and especially, parades, topped off by fireworks exploding across a darkened night sky.

Sometimes, the coal mine operators in our small West Virginia town would give the miners a week off around the July 4th holiday. Families, including mine, would head for the state park or the Greenbrier River for a week of wilderness camping. We'd set up tents on the river bank, and spend the week swimming, fishing, and telling ghost stories around the nightly campfire.

If no vacation was offered, we'd spend the holiday at home. On the evening of July 3rd, we'd have a big picnic in the backyard with relatives and neighbors. My dad always planted a large garden. Part of the July 4th celebration was picking the first ripe tomatoes to layer on grilled cheeseburgers in giant buns slathered with mayonnaise. The first fresh corn was usually ready for picking by then, too. We'd roast it, husks, and all, in a firepit Dad dug in the ground, then drizzle it with my Aunt Kaye's freshly-churned butter. Everyone brought their culinary specialty to share so there were salads, pies, cakes, lemonade, and always, watermelon, which dribbled down our faces and necks onto shirts stained a sticky red. When it got dark, the older kids lit sparklers, and shot-off twinkling fireworks that brightened the night like swarms of fireflies.

Early on the morning of the 4th, we'd head to the nearby town of Rainelle for the big parade. The Veterans of Foreign Wars headed the procession, heads high, boots shiny. The Boy Scouts marched next, carrying the flag, high and proud, grinning as the crowd on both sides of the street stood and cheered. The high school band followed, playing a rousing medley of patriotic songs, led by a bevy of prancing majorettes. Next was a string of antique cars carrying the mayor and other dignitaries. My favorite thing was the floats, decorated with crepe paper in fanciful designs, usually carrying pretty girls-Miss This or That, wearing banners advertising local businesses. When I became a teenager, I rode on one of those floats, all decked out in a yellow, fairy princess gown as Miss Virgil's Barbershop. I kid you not!

As the years went by, Rainelle's 4th of July parade went the way of Virgil's Barbershop-gone forever, but the tradition was carried on by a neighbor city. I never outgrew my love of those celebrations and parades. After I married and moved away, I always tried to be home for what became the July 4th family reunion. The routine was much the same as when I was a child. My brothers and I still got up early, loaded chairs and picnic lunches into cars, and headed off for this much-anticipated adventure, this time dragging husbands, wives, and our own kids.

You had to arrive early to get a shady spot along the parade route. We'd set up our chairs under the trees, break out the snacks and wait impatiently for the firetruck sirens signaling the beginning of the parade. I loved the serendipity of my little kids enjoying the same kind of old-fashioned parade I had loved-the bands, the antique cars, the convertibles carrying beauty queens, and the crepe-paper-decorated floats.

One year, there was an unexpected float at the end of the parade. It was filled with smiling women, all ages, all sizes-waving, tossing candies to the kids on the sidelines, followed by a row of state policemen on motorcycles. The crowd around me stood, clapping and cheering. I squinted to read the sign on the front. It said, **Alderson Women's Prison Trustees.** I learned later they were all to be released that day, having served their time and paid their debt to society. Independence Day had a hopeful, new meaning for them on that sunny 4th of July.

Patriotism Lives

There is a wonderful sameness about 4th of July parades…

- The high school bands, red-faced in 100-degree heat, but high-stepping, with faithful moms running alongside, spritzing the kids with water, and looking as if someone needed to spritz them.
- The awkward, little girl dance troupes, with gangly legs and sparkly costumes, brandishing batons and toothless grins that turn parents and grandparents into lumps of loving goo.
- Acres of Boy and Girl Scouts, resplendent in uniforms plastered with patches and medals.
- Politicians, flashing winning smiles, aimed at gaining votes in the next election.
- Antique cars filled with antique grandmas and grandpas, waving and throwing candy to the kids on the sidelines.
- Fire trucks, sirens blaring, getting more applause and respect in this age of domestic and international terrorism.
- Paper Mache floats, transporting radiant beauty queens in glittering crowns and fairytale gowns.
- A van filled with Special Olympics athletes, getting more applause than the politicians.

The best part of the parade for me is last-everyone in the crowd standing, hats off, hands over hearts, as Old Glory passes by, escorted proudly by the high school drill team, followed by the Veterans of Foreign Wars, in faded uniforms and polished boots. Patriotism, does, indeed, live.

Both of my grandfathers served in World War I, my father in World War II and my husband in Vietnam. I salute all our veterans and all those brave service members still standing guard around the world, so we can attend 4th of July parades.

On the Way to the Greatest State Fair on Earth

Skeletons of *houses past* line the two-lane road. Weeds invade porches where rocking chairs once sat. Shattered windows stare blankly at the blazing June sun. Here and there, a brick chimney rises resolutely from flattened debris. Entire blocks of houses have disappeared as if swept up by alien invaders.

The real invader was water, a one-hundred-year flood, triggered by days of pounding rain that turned tranquil rivers and creeks into roaring predators that carried away everything in their path. As powerful as the ocean, the water lifted houses off foundations and deposited them in the middle of highways, leaving the occupants to be discovered in the wreckage as water receded, looking like broken dolls, arms and legs askew.

Arial photos showed the entire business district of Rainelle, West Virginia, under eight feet of water, roofs barely visible. Eight miles away in the neighboring town of Rupert, houses, vehicles, and bodies floated in the streets, a heart-rending stew of devastation.

The stories were difficult to hear. An elderly couple climbed into their attic to escape. As the water reached them, the husband laid his head on his wife's shoulder and passed away. When rescuers finally arrived, she was still holding his body. A father tied his three children to himself and tried to walk them out of the flood area. The rope came loose and a daughter was washed away, her body found days later, miles downstream.

As we travel along Route 60, my brother, Carl, maintains a continuing commentary, showing me where familiar roads have disappeared as the path of streams was changed and bridges were washed away. I am visiting my hometown on the one-year anniversary of the storm that changed so many lives forever, a storm that was a three-minute blip on the national news, then forgotten by the outside world.

For the residents of this rural coal mining area, however, it has been an unforgettable year of grieving and trying to move on. The scars are everywhere-in the debris of demolished homes and the big, yellow "D" on buildings still awaiting FEMA's bulldozers. My own birthplace is one of those slated for demolition. As we continue our journey, Carl also points out the encouraging signs-small box-like houses on stilts, creating a patchwork landscape along the highway, new grass and flowers in freshly planted yards, vegetable gardens flourishing-change, new life emerging from the destruction.

Our destination is the State Fairgrounds, where a concert will commemorate the lives lost one year ago and recognize the efforts of all those who worked so hard to save their towns and help their neighbors rebuild-from the members of the National Guard who braved flood waters to search and rescue, to the churches and civic clubs who fed and clothed the homeless, to the members of local Mennonite communities who came and stayed for weeks to clear out salvageable homes and help re-build, walking the talk of, "It takes a village..."

As we near the fairgrounds, I search for familiar landmarks ...

- the wooden barns that housed the cows, sheep, and pigs, where we held our noses against the stench to pet the rabbits;

- the rickety grandstand, where, as children, we sprawled on the sun-warmed bleachers, trying desperately to stay awake till dark to watch the fireworks. It wasn't easy to keep weary eyes open, because fair days were long days. We always arrived early, so we could get a good parking spot in the free grassy field adjoining the closer, graveled, paid parking lot.

The fifty cents we saved on parking would buy ten ride tickets for the Ferris Wheel, the Tilt-a-Whirl, or the Carousel. My brothers and I saved our chore and birthday money all year to spend at the fair. We were each given a dollar, but that had to buy food for all day-corn dogs on sticks for fifteen cents, fries in paper cups for a dime, and cotton candy or candied apples for a nickel.

We wandered through the food booths, looking at everything, pricing everything, deciding where we could get the most goodies for our buck. They were hard decisions. The aroma of buttered popcorn mingled with the scent of batter sizzling in hot fat, just waiting to be coated with powdered sugar and devoured. Cotton candy floated up from stainless steel vats and was wound onto paper cones, coating our noses and mouths with sticky goo. By day's end, the clean, fresh straw that covered the dirt walkway around the carnival was also coated with abandoned cotton candy goo, sticking to our tennis shoes.

Our parents marched us past the side-show tents, never allowing us to go in to see the Bearded Lady or the Man with Two Heads or the Siamese Twins, joined at the chest. The barker's cries of, "Come in! See the five-hundred-pound lady!" were ignored and we were dragged away from the brightly painted posters, but not before we stole a peep through a small slit in the tent.

The carnival rides required more decisions. We were each given fifteen tickets, to last all day, so we had to choose carefully. Did we use up three tickets on the roller-coaster or ride the merry-go-round three times? Tough choices! I would spread my ride tickets out during the day but my brothers would quickly run from ride to ride and then beg for my tickets. I didn't share.

By evening, and fireworks time, we were tired puppies, sometimes with aching tummies from all the greasy food and sweets. As we waited in the grandstand, the umm-pa-pa of the calliope, combined with the barker's cries and the shouts of, "Bingo!" in the Games of Chance tent, all melded together in a mesmerizing muddle of voices and music that lulled us to sleep. But when the crash, bang of the fireworks started, we were wide awake, and thrilled by the spectacle of dazzling star-bursts and spinning rockets that illuminated the night sky.

Tired feet dragged as we joined the crowds searching for their cars. I clutched my doll-on-a-stick that I had spent my last twenty-five cents on. She was so pretty, in her feather dress with matching pink headband and tiny high heels, clutching a sparkling silver cane. We all tumbled into Dad's old Oldsmobile and were fast sleep before the car had inched its way out of the packed parking lot.

Now, approaching what used to be the grassy parking area behind the barns, nothing was recognizable. Carl was explaining that all the old wooden fair buildings, including the grandstand, had been inundated with water, leveled and replaced with steel structures, joined by concrete paths. Nothing remained, not even the blinking red, white, and blue neon sign that could be seen for blocks, welcoming visitors to **THE GREATEST STATE FAIR ON EARTH!**

I closed my eyes and could still see that sign, smell the hay from the barns, taste the sweetness of the cotton candy, and feel the umm-pa-pa beat of the calliope, pulsing through my heart.

Summertime On The River

In the small West Virginia coal mining town where I grew up, money was scarce and vacations were either visits to my grandparents in the western part of the state or camping trips. The coal mines usually closed for two weeks in July, so miners' families would pack up and head for the Greenbrier River. There were great parks on the river, but we couldn't afford the $5-a-week fee, so we would wilderness camp. My dad would go a week early and put up the tents to stake out our campsite in the woods before all the other families converged on the same area.

My mom worked for two weeks ahead of time, packing and cooking to prepare for our week away. Our tents didn't have floors in them so she put tarps on the ground, then added throw rugs on top of that. All five of us had cots with blankets and pillows so you can imagine how packed the car was by the time we crammed in camp stoves, fold-up tables, cooking utensils, water buckets, ice chests, and food. Added to that were innertubes for floating in the river and extra shoes for wading because the river had a rocky bottom with sharp rocks. The last thing stuffed into the car was the first aid kit for cuts, bruises, and snake bites. Yes, there were snakes in the woods, in the river, and on several occasions, in our tent.

It took a full day to set up camp. Dad had to stretch rain tarps over the table where Mom would cook and we would eat. There was another table with a water bucket and dipper plus a pan for hand washing. There were no toilets, so a space had to be set up inside a small tent for a slop jar. It was emptied twice a day into a trench Dad dug several yards from the campsite.

I would awaken in the mornings to the mouth-watering aroma of bacon sizzling in the big iron skillet. We would toast slices of bread over the campfire to dip into soft-cooked eggs. Lunch was bologna with mustard or peanut butter and jelly sandwiches. Dinner was grilled hamburgers or hot dogs seared over the fire, served in buns with Mom's homemade chili and baked beans. It seemed like she was always cooking, when she wasn't keeping an eye on us while we floated or swam in the clear, icy river. Usually, she went into the water with us, swimming alongside or teaching my younger brothers to swim. My Dad was always fishing. When successful, dinner was battered fish with fried potatoes, and fresh corn, roasted in the coals of the campfire.

At night, the kerosene lanterns were lit to keep the bugs away. We'd play cards or monopoly, and toast mash-mallows over the campfire. My dad loved telling ghost stories, complete with sound effects which would send my youngest brother running into the tent, to hide under his covers.

Other families and relatives camped in the same area, so there were always cousins and other kids to play with. The moms switched off guard duty. I made friends during those summers with kids who are still my old friends today. Over time, our family graduated to better tents with zippers and floors, but the routine was still basically the same-my mom always working. As I grew old enough to appreciate all she did, I asked if she had ever felt over-worked and under-paid on those summer trips. She was genuinely surprised at the question.

Her response, "Those are my some of my fondest family memories, all of us snuggled in a cozy tent, the three of you still giggling as we all fell asleep."

Ghosts and Goblins

Halloween was a family affair when I was growing up. Costumes were homemade, sometimes created on Halloween Day from whatever we happened to have around the house. Ghosts were easy, made from an old sheet or sometimes crepe paper, by just cutting out eyes and a mouth. My brothers sometimes went as cowboys because they always had cowboy hats, guns, and holsters. I always wanted to be a princess. I'd wear an old nightgown of my mom's, cut down to size, topped with a construction paper crown decorated with fake jewels.

We lived on a busy highway with no safe neighborhood streets for trick or treating. My mom would dress up, and escort us house to house. My dad was in-charge-of handing out candy as other families came to the door. He always dressed up too. When we returned from our visits to neighbors, we would dump our loot to see who had gotten the best stuff. Apples and oranges were booed and passed over as we dived into Double Bubble Gum, Fireballs, Dum Dums, Black Taffy, Candy Cigarettes, and my favorite, Candy Necklaces.

My daughter, Shannon, was born on Oct. 30. The list of Halloween birthday party themes and games through the years was endless-from "Pin the nose on the ghost," at age four, to painting pumpkins at age twelve, to painting Mary Kay make-up faces at age fourteen. When she graduated to boy/girl pizza parties at age sixteen, I was relieved because I was totally out of brilliant party ideas.

My husband, Don, loved Halloween. He went all out, trying to frighten the little kids. He had an ugly carved wooden mask we had brought home from Hawaii, with fangs and scraggly hair, that he would wear with a long, black gown, and bear claw slippers. By-the-way, he wore those same bear claw slippers when we got married. What can I say-the man had a quirky sense of humor.

One Halloween night, he sat on a stool on the sidewalk in front of my townhouse in his mask, gown, and slippers, offering candy from a bear's skull. How many takers do you think he had? Kids would come close, then turn around and run back to warn their friends, "Don't go there! Scary monster!" He finally had to take the mask off so the kids would come and get the candy.

The costume was so great, he won a prize that year for the Scariest Costume at the big Halloween party at the Hampton Air and Space Museum. I dressed as a belly dancer and we went as Beauty and the Beast. We even made the papers as the Best Costumed Couple. Ahh, such fame!

During covid, my neighborhood debated whether to cancel "trick or treating." We finally decided we would make packets of treats and leave them in bowls on the doorstep so each child could just pick one up, eliminating all those little hands mangling and contaminating the goodies. Halloween must go on!

Rulers of the Night

They pierce the gloom with eerie smile,
greet visitors with glee.
Ambassadors of fun and fright,
wish only to run free.
Round, orange heads, no legs attached,
decapitated ghosts.
They fear anticipated fate,
as pumpkin soup with toast.

Travel with Me

Part 4

Been There - Done That
Happy Dance!

Paradise Found

My husband, Don, and I love to travel. One of our favorite spots is tiny Cooper Island in the British Virgin Islands. Our second trip there was a few days after the 9/11 attack. It was like going from hell into paradise. We could hardly believe so much beauty and tranquility could exist in the same world with the devastation and fear we had left behind. Even the plane trip was surreal. We changed planes in Boston, walking through an airport protected by armed National Guardsmen onto a plane that had more flight attendants than passengers. We were uneasy about flying, but decided the precautions probably made it a safer-than-usual time to travel. So off we went, from Boston to Puerto Rico, to the island of Tortola, where a boat, captained by Chris, who co-owns the Cooper Island Beach Club, picked us up and whisked us to the island.

The Beach Club is very private-six yellow and pink cottages nestled in the trees, an outdoor gourmet restaurant, and a thatch-roofed hut with a seldom-open boutique which sells swim wear and postcards. There is no electricity, no phone except for emergencies, no television, no roads, no hassles. Our frig, stove and lights are gas powered. The water for our shower, which is on the back porch, is desalinated sea water, solar heated. We have a well-stocked bookcase and a cassette player. But we usually prefer the music of the sea.

Awake at 6 a.m. I prop up on my pillows in my comfy bed and watch a rosy dawn emerge from the sea. Into my bathing suit and out the door for our morning seashell search along the water's edge of our deserted beach. The sea is warm as bath water and deep azure blue. Palm trees nod in the breeze and melodic bird songs punctuate the silence.

Don and I share fruit and cereal on our porch and watch the sailboats come to life in the distance. A tiny hummingbird flits from branch to branch of the Seagrape tree in our front yard. Hermit crabs drag their shells over the sand. Tiny lizards entertain us with their mighty leaps from rock to rock, sailing effortlessly through the air. The breeze, fragrant with salt and exotic flowers, intoxicates.

Some mornings, we kayak around the island, exploring the lagoons. Other days, we hike to the top, where some energetic soul has cut crude steps into the hillside and built a columned viewing area at the summit. From there, we can look down on the other side of the island. Below is a homestead with a vegetable garden, goats and chickens, and a dock, all belonging to the native family who are the lucky owners of this paradise.

Today, Don snorkels and I write, savoring the cool, quiet morning. Lunch at our open-air cafe is a daily adventure, enjoyed at white tables under an awning that shields us from the 90+ noontime sun. Bathing suits are the attire of choice. We linger over iced tea in large, sweating pitchers and share conversation with our friends, Becky and Jim, who first introduced us to this tiny island, and our new friends, Caz and Bob, who are honeymooners from Pittsburgh. The only other guest is a young redhead, named Kate, who leaves early every day to go diving, and who has, so far, declined to join our friendly lunch and dinner group. We are the only guests on the island.

The staff outnumbers us. Curt, from Trinidad, is the manager who can solve any problem, and cooks special desserts for us, just because he likes us. Antoine grins shyly as he carries the luggage and works around the grounds. Brandon is the tall, lanky handyman, who fixes everything. Liz serves our meals and reads Harry Potter books in every spare moment. Wayne waits tables and charms us with his dry, British wit. Nate has a smile that would warm the hardest of hearts, and is also a Harry Potter fan. Last, but certainly not least, Chris is the tall Brit who co-owns the Beach Club and seems to be everywhere at once. The staff lives in a dormitory-style building built into the hillside above the beach, hidden by cactus and flowering trees.

Afternoons are lazy. We nap or read or play in the crystal-clear water with schools of brightly-colored fish. Each day, the snorkelers compare notes about their sightings-a trio of octopus, a 6 ft. barracuda, a giant ray. Yesterday, the excitement was on shore, rather than in the water. Don picked up a small, black plastic oil bottle on the beach and left it on the ground near our stairs. Within a half hour, it was surrounded by dozens of hermit crabs, dragging their shell houses. They came and they stayed! They were there all day and all night, apparently worshiping at the shrine of the empty oil bottle.

As the day begins to fade, we ooh and ahh over the breath-taking sunset from our porch. We sip wine and nibble cheese and crackers as the sun settles into the sea, finger-painting the sky in glorious hues of scarlet and fuchsia with ribbons of gold. As the last trace of color fades into the horizon, we amble off to dinner, dressed in our most formal t-shirts and shorts.

On clear nights, the awning is rolled back. We dine by candlelight under the stars on delicious Caribbean specialties and scrumptious desserts. We pig out, agreeing that food with friends has no calories. We save morsels for Cody, the green-eyed island cat, who, every day, waits politely and patiently under the table for treats.

On the way back to our cottage, we wander out to the end of the pier to star gaze, soaking in the beauty of the night sky and the peaceful solitude surrounding us. Thoughts of our flight home tomorrow are clouded by the knowledge that we are returning to the aftermath of the horrific attacks of 9/11, just two weeks earlier. We wonder when, if ever, we will be privileged to be this free, this safe again, and together with our best friends.

We walk home in the darkness, guided by our torches (Brit for flashlight), and are in bed by 9. The moonlight streaming through our open bedroom window is bright enough to read by, but reading doesn't last long. The surf crashing on the shore lulls us quickly to sleep. I drift off, grateful for one more perfect day in paradise.

WESTWARD HO!

Sights And Sounds Of The Southwest

My friend, Kaye, and I like to travel. Recently, we decided to visit a girlfriend, Vivien, in Cottonwood, Arizona, for an extraordinary trip through the Southwest. Join us...

Six lanes of traffic in each direction, sizzle in the heat as we leave the Phoenix airport on the first day of our Southwest adventure.

Saguaro cactus replace tall buildings as we happily depart the city. Did you know it takes ten years for a Saguaro cactus to reach an inch in height? By seventy, it can grow to six feet tall but won't produce its first arm until it is 95-100 years of age. Understandably, they are protected as a wondrous species.

A candlelit Chapel in the Rocks fills us with serenity as we soak in the beauty and spirituality of the red rocks of Sedona. It has been my heart home since my first visit years ago.

The panorama of blues, burgundy, and pinks of the Painted Desert at dusk has inspired artists for generations. We take photos, but they disappoint, not quite capturing the array of colors.

The Petrified Forest is a graveyard of fallen tree trunks, now calcified into a rainbow of crystals. Near-by are the petroglyphs of Newspaper Rock and the ruins of Puerco Pueblo. Paleontologists continue to try and piece together the stories of its residents.

We travel through Navajo lands on our way to Canyon de Chelly. Squalid houses on barren land speak to the poverty of these Native Americans. I question the old tires on the flat roofs. I am told the monsoon winds rip off the tin roofs. The tires hold them down. The contrast between the tiny homes and the majestic sandstone cliffs and spires of the nearby canyon is striking.

Monument Valley is a magnificent red-sand desert bordering Arizona and Utah, known for its towering sandstone buttes. We are told we can drive through a section of it. We are not told the road is rutted out, and, in some places, covered with six inches of sand. Our rental car wheezes and bumps but fortunately, we make it without having to get out and push. Later, we sit on the porch of our little rental house and watch the sun set over the buttes of the red valley. Unforgettable!

Jerome is an old copper mining town, perched on the side of a hill. The houses slip down the mountain about an inch a year. The ghost town has become an artist mecca, filling the old houses with something better than copper-gorgeous jewelry, pottery, and paintings. On top of the hill is a huge structure known as The Asylum. Constructed of steel and concrete to withstand the winds, it was once a hospital for the 3000+ men who toiled in the mines. Later, it was a mental hospital, and now a hotel and restaurant. The narrow, dark halls, period furniture, and paintings are background for stories of ghosts that do, we're told, walk the halls at night. We were there for lunch, so didn't get to meet them.

The Cicadas awakened me in the cowboy town of Prescott, serenading us with their unusual song. It repels birds, saving the large insects from being eaten. They can produce sound in-excess-of 120 decibels at close range, which approaches the pain threshold for human ears. As we wandered around Prescott's quaint downtown area with its courthouse square, Whiskey Row saloons and interesting shops, the Cicadas sang on.

The grandeur of the Grand Canyon defies description. The South Rim drive has pull-offs that allow you to walk to the edge and take pictures that don't come anywhere near capturing its magnificence. The colors change from lavender to blue to gray to pink, depending on the light. The canyon also makes people a little crazy. They perch their babies on the rocky rim and step away to take photos. They fly drones into the abyss to get a closer view, even though it's illegal to do so. They climb over barriers and hang over the side of the canyon even though signs clearly say, "Thou shalt not…" Several people have died there this summer from their own foolishness.

I had never seen the canyon at sunset, so in the evening, we rushed to the Watch Tower to thrill at the spectacle, along with dozens of other tourists. The temperature dropped from 90 degrees to 40 in minutes as the crimson light left the canyon in darkness. We walked back to our car in silence, awed by the wonder of it all.

The Elephants Who Came to Dinner

Mfuwe Lodge in South Luang National Park, Zambia, is spread beneath a magnificent canopy of ebony and mahogany trees. Its thatched buildings are arranged around the banks of two lagoons where an endless stream of wildlife wanders freely. A wild mango tree has lured generations of elephants every November, long before the lodge was built.

The first year Mfuwe opened for business, the elephants made it clear this betrayal of their space would not change their route or intentions. They walked into the open-air lobby with no warning, shuffled through and out into the courtyard to feast on the mangoes. Don't you wish you could have seen the look on the face of the receptionist that day? Every year since, the elephants' sojourn to the mango tree draws crowds of tourists to the lodge. The elephants ignore them, intent on only one thing-mangoes. When the mangoes are gone, so are the elephants, parading back through the lobby and into the wilderness.

According to the lodge owners, the group that makes the annual stroll through the lobby represents several generations of one elephant family, including their matriarch, Wonky Tusk, and the youngest addition, Lord Wellington, who was a baby when he made his first lobby march. Baby elephants are incredibly protected by their female family. Imagine the trust level that elephant mom demonstrated, bringing her child into a building inhabited by humans. Who knew mangoes were that enticing?

STRANGE THINGS I KNOW ABOUT AMERICA

A coast to coast, 60-day, 9000-mile motor-home adventure left me with a collection of strange things I now know about our country. Here are just a few.

- In Mitchell, S. D., there is a magnificent palace covered in corn kernels and multi-hued corn husks. It is rebuilt by the townspeople every year with a remarkable new design as an expression of pride in their farming community.

- The Barbed Wire Museum in LaCrosse, Kansas, features more than 500 different types of the prickly stuff. Who knew barbed wire had its own museum?

- Only Rome, Italy, has more fountains than Kansas City, Missouri. It also claims the dubious honor of having produced America's first shopping center.

- Once it was illegal to serve ice cream on cherry pie in Kansas. Nobody could tell me why.

- If you're having a less-than-ideal family vacation and want to lose the kids for a while, the corn maze in Buhler, Kansas is the place to go. They do insist that you collect them before dark.

- In the Oregon Vortex, in Gold Hill, Oregon, balls roll uphill, short people appear taller and vice-versa. Engineers have conducted over 14,000 experiments in the House of Mystery, and can only explain the phenomenon as a "whirlpool of invisible energy."

- In South Dakota, a 563-foot statue of Chief Crazy Horse, seated on a horse, is beginning to emerge from a granite mountain, not far from Mt. Rushmore. The Polish sculptor died in 1982 after spending fifty years of his life working on the carving. His children and grandchildren are carrying on the work, funding the project from their own and privately-donated funds, carving out pieces of the mountain as they earn the money to do so. Slowly, surely, they are blasting, drilling, and chiseling the pride of the Sioux people into the mountain.

- Strange signs abound as you travel state to state. My favorite was in Shady Cove, Oregon. It proclaimed in huge letters, "Thanks for coming. Love Ya!"

WELL-BEHAVED WOMEN RARELY MAKE HISTORY

Wallace, Idaho, population 784, is a historic mining town. It has long been known as the Silver Capitol of the World, producing 1.2 billion ounces of silver since 1884. It is the only place on earth where more than a billion ounces of silver were mined in one-hundred years. Every downtown building is on the National Register of Historic Places. When the Interstate Highway system was completed in 1991, it had to go over the town, not through it, to protect the original buildings, including the Oasis Bordello Museum.

The Oasis opened in 1895, when there were two hundred men to every woman in Wallace. Survival was the name of the game. If your vision of a Wild West brothel includes gunslingers and glamorous women in corsets, a visit to the Oasis might alter your view. The bordello kept its doors open until 1988. That's right, 1988.

While Nancy Reagan was telling America, "Just say no to drugs," the ladies of the Oasis were saying "yes," to any man in Wallace with twenty bucks. When they fled the bordello in fear of an F. B. I. raid in 1988, among the things left behind was a chalk board with a list of all their regulars which included most of the male population of Wallace. The ladies never returned and the current owners preserved the rooms exactly as they were abandoned on that night, providing a view of the 1980's through the unique prism of the prostitutes, right down to the J. C. Penney catalogues on the coffee table and the video store rental list taped to the kitchen wall.

Visitors to the brothel climbed a set of creaky steps and entered through a triple-dead-bolted door. The madam played Atari all night and her console TV in the living room is still piled with her favorite cartridges - Breakout, Space Invaders, and Pac-Man.

Nearby, the brothel's price list is taped to the wall for easy reference, written on a sheet of yellow tablet paper, broken down by sex act and timed to the minute."Eight minutes, fifteen dollars, straight, no frills." "Bubble bath, half hour, fifty dollars," etc.

The linen closet in the hall was lined with four long shelves, piled with small, fuzzy rugs.

The client was encouraged to take one into the bedroom with him and put it on the bed, making clean-up easier and faster. In the broom closet, along with bottles of Scope, cans of Lysol and carpet cleaner, were several dozen red light bulbs for the lamps in the bedrooms.

In the prostitutes' rooms, the museum displays showroom dummies in lingerie left behind when the women fled. Stockings, bras, and frilly panties hang from mirrors and lamps. Vanities are cluttered with cans of hair spray, boxes of press-on nails, and an occasional bottle of NyQuil or box of Vivarin. Each room has a wash bucket, a paper cup dispenser, and a can of air freshener. In the only bathroom are seven medicine cabinets- one for each resident. The bathroom has a tub and toilet, but no shower or shower curtain. It served the needs of all the women in the house.

The kitchen doubled as the nerve center of the business. On the counter was a line of wind-up timers, one for each room. When the bell rang, the maid knocked on the door and said, "Time's up!" A drawer under the counter was filled with gears and springs. The women were so busy, they wore out the timers. Unlike the women of the 1895 Oasis, who traded their bodies for food and a roof over their heads, the prostitutes at the Oasis in 1988 made as much as $2000 a week. The 1980's madam regularly donated money to the community for schools, parks, and was secretly liked and respected by most of the residents.

The town of Wallace at first objected to the bordello being turned into a museum but now trumpets its sex trade heritage to tourists with businesses such as the Red-Light Garage, and The Best Little Hair House Beauty Salon. Several of the women who worked at the Oasis have returned over the years to visit the museum and contribute their own survival stories to the archives. In thirty-seven years, the women of the Oasis have gone from shocking to historic.

Since the beginnings of our country, women have joined the ranks of historical figures by doing things that were as shocking in their time, as the women of the Oasis were in theirs.

In 1607, European women left their homes and traveled across the ocean to the Jamestown Colony to marry men they had never seen and civilize a wilderness.

Victoria Woodhull was the first woman to run for President of the United States in 1871.

She was ridiculed and her life threatened. It would be one hundred thirty-seven years before Hillary Clinton followed in her footsteps. She, too, was ridiculed and threatened. But, like Victoria, she persisted.

Two siblings, nicknamed the Birth Control Sisters were arrested in 1916 for opening a birth control clinic in Brooklyn. Others would follow their example with the same results, year after year, in small towns and big cities around the country. Anti-abortion laws were not struck down until 1973, then rescinded, fifty years later in 2023. Brave women are still fighting every day to regain those reproductive rights.

There were other historic firsts that were hard-won and a long time coming.

Sandra Day O'Connor became the first female Supreme Court Justice in 1981, despite ugly comments that women weren't smart enough to be appointed to that lofty position.

When Astronaut Sally Ride became the first American woman to travel in space in 1983, there were mutterings that women were not strong enough to explore the new frontier. Both Ride and O'Connor proved the nay sayers wrong.

In 2014, a teenager, Malala Yousadzai, was awarded the Nobel Peace Prize, and walked into the history books, after surviving an assassination attempt because of her outspoken battle for women's educational and human rights.

Women continue to make history today, as they step up in record numbers to run for public offices and organize protests around the country, continuing the fight for human rights, gun control, equal wages, and the environment. The determined women of the "Me Too" movement exposed sexual abuse and began the battle to stop it, coming full circle from the desperate women of the 1895 Oasis.

No doubt, well-behaved women do sometimes make history, but more often, it is the rebels who fight, struggle, and sometimes die, who carry their stories and their causes into the history books.

SCENES FROM THE VATICAN, APRIL 26, 2025

A sea of cardinals in red robes with white pointed hats, like crested red birds.

Hundreds of priests in white with red beauty queen ribbons across their chests.

Priests in sun-protecting ball caps, removed quickly as cameras zoom in.

Kings, presidents, all in dress code black, except for US president in bright blue.

Loud applause for Ukraine's President Volodymyr Zelensky, as he enters.

Groups of teens, on their phones, continuing to do what teens do worldwide.

Exotic Eastern visitors in crowns, bejeweled turbans, and gold-threaded brocade.

Nuns-where were the holy sisters in the rows of church elite? None to be seen.

An Indian elder in native regalia, including an elaborate Aztec headdress.

Guards in clown-like yellow/blue uniforms with balloon trousers, red plumed hats.

250,000 somber citizens, behind metal barriers with picnic lunches, crying babies.

Secret Service agents with obviously large ear buds, staring intently at the crowds.

Ancient Mass conducted with ornate goblets and golden vessels under a tent.

Clouds of incense floating through the air, enough to purify a small country.

Tolling of the bells to commemorate the life of Franciscus, the People's Pope,

laid to rest in a simple wooden coffin at Rome's Basilica di Santa Maris Maggiore.

Amen.

My Fantasy Life

A rosy dawn emerges from the sea, trailing silver across the azure water. Palm trees nod in the breeze. Melodic bird song punctuates the silence. I feel as if I own the island…and I do, thanks to my best-selling travel book which rose to #1 on the New York Times Best Seller List, and the three equally successful sequels that followed.

Sharon's Island is our family summer home and my year-round private paradise. As soon as school is out, Son, Steven, wife, Amy, and grandkids, Adaline, Emma, and Zachary jump on the family jet and join me here. They operate a wintertime bed and breakfast in the ski area of the Shenandoah Mountains, so look forward to holidays and summers in the sun. Daughter, Shannon, and spouse, A. J., run a non-profit environmental organization in Williamsburg, VA. Our great new wi-fi system allows them to join us for summer months and long holidays.

Each family designed their own home on the island. Steven and Amy's is huge with playrooms and bedrooms for their kids, plus extras for the "Big Brother, Big Sister" kids they sponsor every summer. Steven wanted to pay back, because he never forgot what that organization meant to him as a young, fatherless teen. Their compound has a pool, plus basketball court, and soccer field, so my grandkids can keep up with their practice during the summer. It's like a noisy summer camp all the time.

Shannon and A. J. wanted a small cottage in a secluded part of the island with an outdoor shower and indoor hot tub. Their extravagance was a chef's kitchen, complete with gadgets galore. They love to cook and treat us to gourmet meals every Saturday night.

My house is close to the beach so I can beachcomb before breakfast, and watch spectacular nightly sunsets from my high-perched porch. My splurge was a state-of-the-art movie theatre which draws the grandkids almost every evening. We all take turns sharing dinners or lunches on our tree-shaded porches and patios. The island is large with tropical forests to explore. The warm, sparkling water teems with orange, cobalt, and yellow striped fish. Dolphin play nearby. An instructor comes once a week to give all the kids scuba and kayaking lessons. My late husband, Don, would be happy about that. Those were two of his favorite hobbies. He introduced me to this lush island. We never dreamed then, I would someday own it.

When the family goes home in late August, my busy months start. During September and October, I bring in great authors and poets who teach workshops for writers who flock here from all over the world to stay in the dorm/classroom complex that crowns the top of the only hill on the island. The hilltop compound also has a staff dorm and a completely equipped underground shelter for refuge from tropical storms.

Steven, Shannon, spouses, and kids return to the island for Thanksgiving week and we all spend Christmas in the Shenandoah bed and breakfast. They ski. I shop. In January, the parade of friends escaping winter snow and ice begins, and continues through March. I never thought of myself as an innkeeper, but apparently, I'm a good one. They all keep coming back. My multi-cultural house staff is composed of college students who work here to earn money for tuition. They change sheets, clean, and cook delicious meals for my guests and me. I always select at least one budding chef to join the staff. Most of them come back every summer or winter, until they graduate. They become extended family. I'm like the "old woman who lived in a shoe."

Between visitors, I write. Books and poems seem to create themselves in the solitude of my third-floor crow's nest, overlooking the sea. I don't miss the mainland with its noise and increasingly angry citizens. I do watch the news occasionally, but feel far removed from the turmoil. It was always my dream to live on a tropical island. Writing makes it so.

Life Lessons

Part 5

Been There - Done That
Happy Dance!

All I Need To Know, I Learned From The Easter Bunny

Don't put all your eggs in one basket.

Everyone needs a friend who is all ears.

There's no such thing as too much candy.

All work, no play, can make you a basket case.

A cute tail attracts a lot of attention.

Everyone is entitled to a bad hare day.

Some body parts should be floppy.

Keep your paws off other people's jelly beans.

Good things come in small, sugar-coated packages.

The grass is always greener in someone else's basket.

To show your true colors, you must come out of your shell.

Every day, let happy thoughts multiply like bunnies.

Letter To My Ten-Year-Old Self

Dear Sharon,

Congratulations to you and your best friend, Sandra, for winning second place in the county talent contest. The two of you have been singing duets since first grade, so, of course you wanted to be in the contest, even though you were the youngest contestants. You worked hard, rehearsing after school with cousin Hazel on special choreography. You were so cute in your cowgirl outfits-jeans, red plaid shirts and cowboy hats. *Ricochet Romance* was a great song choice. The harmony was perfect. I really don' t think anyone noticed when you couldn' t get the toy gun out of the holster for the grand finale. I' m sure nobody could tell your heart was beating out of your chest with nervousness the whole time. Mom and Daddy didn' t think the two of you were good enough be in the show. Maybe they were trying to protect you from disappointment. But you noticed they were grinning when you won. Mom didn' t even scrub off the little bit of lipstick cousin Hazel had sneaked onto your lips just before you went on stage.

You were disappointed you didn' t win first place. You got the loudest applause. It was hard for you to understand why the pretty majorette won, even though she kept dropping her baton and bending over to pick it up. Eventually, you' ll figure all that out, and it will kick off a life-long Women's Lib campaign. You will become a strong, successful woman, and you will choose a profession that allows you to help other women be successful too. Sandra will be your lifelong friend, and don't worry. For you, the music never ends. Someday, you will sing with a remarkable award-winning barbershop chorus. This time, there will be a first-place win. I wish I could say to you at ten, "Be brave. Stand up for yourself. Most of all, be patient. You will be loved and life will be good."

Self

THINGS EVERY WOMAN SHOULD HAVE AND KNOW TODAY

Every Woman Should Have…

- One old love she can imagine going back to, and one who reminds her of how far she's come.

- Enough money within her control to move out and rent a place of her own, even if she never wants to or needs to. Something perfect to wear if a prospective employer or the date of her dreams wants to see her in an hour.

- A youth she's content to leave behind, and a past juicy enough to retell proudly in her old age.

- A set of screwdrivers, a cordless drill, and a black lace bra.

- One friend who always makes her laugh and one who lets her cry.

- A good piece of furniture not previously owned by anyone else in her family.

- Eight matching plates, wine glasses with stems, and a recipe for a meal that will make her guests feel honored.

- A resume that is not the slightest bit padded.

- Money set aside to fund her old age.

- A feeling of control over her destiny.

Every Woman Should Know...

- How to fall in love without losing herself.
- How to quit a job; break up with a lover; and confront a friend without ruining a friendship.
- When to try harder and when to walk away.
- How to have a good time at a party she didn't choose to attend.
- How to ask for what she wants in a way that makes it most likely she'll get it.
- That she can't change the length of her calves or the nature of her parents.
- That her childhood may not have been perfect, but it's over.
- What she would and would not do for love.
- How to live alone, even if she doesn't like it.
- What she can and can't accomplish in a day, a month, a year.
- Where to go when her soul needs soothing.

Spring Cleaning – Closet Closure

Marie somebody or other took the country by storm by declaring we should only keep the things that "bring us joy." Everything else should GO! When I heard that, my thought was, well, on a bad day, that could be a sloppy husband or a disobedient kid, or even, the dog, when he chews up your best slippers. They are definitely not "bringing us joy" at that moment. There's also that other rule, "If you haven't used it in a year, off to the dump or the thrift store."

During a recent spring closet cleaning in my office, I discovered lots of things that should have been long gone under one or both of those rules…

…A small box of cassette tapes of my son's piano recital, age 10, and my daughter's performance in a speech contest, age 12. He is now fifty-six and can only play chopsticks. She is fifty and hates public speaking. I can now play those tapes and say, "See, you should have kept practicing!"

…A box of old photos from the 70's of my Sweet Adeline barbershop chorus. Our show theme one year was "Fairy Tales," and we were all in different costumes depicting our favorite fairy tale, cartoon, or Disney character. I was in a tiny Wonder Woman costume that barely covered my 110 lb. skinny frame. Well, maybe that could have gone out. Today's comparison is pretty depressing. Although, I am still trying to BE Wonder Woman, just without the costume.

…A shoebox overflowing with old birthday and Christmas cards from people whose names I barely remember. Yes, I did look at every single one and I'm glad I did. Hidden among the throw-aways, a birthday card from my grandfather the year he died, and tucked inside, a dollar bill. He sent one to each grandchild every year, even after we'd grown up.

...Two plastic storage boxes full of gloves and mittens with no mates. Maybe I thought they would find their way home someday? No joy there-gone!

...My high school and college yearbooks, certainly not used in a year or twenty+ years. Do they bring me joy? Sure, remembering the friendships, the innocence, and the fun, but joy tinged with sadness that so many of those friends are gone now.

...Folders of yellowed newspaper clippings about celebrities, world events-Kennedy's assassination; Jane Fonda protesting the Vietnam War; planes flying into the Trade Center; an entire folder of stories about Elvis Presley's death. Yes, I did love him, I confess! Is there joy in those souvenirs of the past? Not exactly, but they are potent reminders of trials and tribulations we all survived together. I didn't save any clippings about the multitudes of people, worldwide, who fell victim to the coronavirus. But I did write a book about it. We can now look back and say we survived that trial and tribulation, too.

So, Marie, I opened a lot of doors to the past this week that wouldn't have been there if I'd listened to your advice. Those walks down memory lane brought me joy, some sadness, some closure, but most importantly, the reassurance that bad times do pass and we do move on.

LIKE SAND THROUGH AN HOUR-GLASS
(20 years since 9/11)

Life slips through our fingers like sand–five years, ten–suddenly it's twenty years since the terrorists of 9/11 stole the lives of so many, as well as the childhoods of their children.

Journalists share tales of redemption–sons who honored their fathers by becoming firemen, apprenticing in the same station, wearing their dad's hat into their first fire.

We hear stories of people who worked in the towers and managed to escape, becoming guardians for their lost friends' children, raising them, loving them, never forgetting.

Thousands of wives, husbands, mothers, dads, grieved without closure; woke up each day to put one foot in front of the other, regroup, rebuild family branches, like lost Octopus limbs.

We can't bring back those lost family members, but we can support survivors and workers who still suffer from the tocsins generated that day, and during the weeks, months that followed. We can push our government to honor these heroes and victims by willingly increasing medical benefits instead of forcing them from sick beds to fight for every penny of assistance.

We can remember, life does slip through our fingers like sand through an hourglass, while being grateful that we still have both time and life–we, all the fortunate survivors of 9/11.

September, 2021

As We Remember

It was September 11, 2001, 9 a.m. I was working in my home office when the phone rang. My friend, Barbara, was shrieking, "Turn on the television! Turn on the television!" I did, in time to see the second plane hit the New York Trade Center. I didn't move from that spot for hours. I couldn't believe what I was seeing.

I had more than a concerned citizen's interest when another attack flashed on the screen. Flight 77 had hit the Pentagon. My heart nearly jumped out of my chest. I knew my son, Steven, had an appointment there that morning. He, at that time, was an investigator for the government, with a morning meeting scheduled at the Pentagon. I wouldn't know until much later in the day, that he had gotten caught in early morning traffic, making him late for that appointment and probably saving his life. One hundred-twenty-five others who were working at the Pentagon that day were not so lucky. Twenty-seven-hundred would die in the Twin Towers, including more than four hundred emergency responders. Forty-eight more would perish on Flight 93 that went down near Shanksville, PA, after a heroic effort by passengers to storm the cockpit, keeping the plane from reaching its D.C. destination.

I waited and watched in horror that day, and I prayed. Steven was unable to reach me immediately to let me know he was okay. The D. C. phone systems had crashed as people like me tried frantically to reach loved ones. He couldn't get home 'til that afternoon, because roads were immediately shut down, stranding thousands of commuters. It felt like the longest day of my life.

Each year since that horrendous day, we remember those we lost by reading their names at the site of the Twin Towers Memorial. I watch with grief and gratitude, and then call my son to tell him I love him.

The Circle Of Life

As I begin to acknowledge the reality of the "O" word (O meaning old) as it relates to myself, I see life as that O, a circle, beginning as a blank page and ultimately, ending with that same blank page, the slate wiped clean.

My mother died a few years ago. I helped to clear out her house. My brothers and I were born and raised there. My mother lived there for seventy years. The walls should scream with the laughter and tears of all those years. But they stand silent, antiseptically clean, waiting for the next chapter. All that happened there, between beginning and end, seems to have been neatly erased. If all trace of us is erased at the end, what is the purpose of the middle of life-between the beginning and ending? Think about this. We begin life dependent on others. Most likely, we will end it dependent in some way. Most of us start our adult lives penniless. Too often, we end our story in that same way.

So, is the in-between meant to be a time to accumulate money and things? Is it a time to acquire knowledge and wisdom, and are they the same thing? Is it a time to search for that perfect love, that soul mate who will supposedly complete us? Do we find happiness and the meaning of life in all these things or none of them, and what, if anything, do we leave behind?

I hear my mother's words coming out my mouth all the time. I notice my children repeating their step-father's sayings. I believe, what is left behind is not what is accumulated or taught, but rather, what is **caught** by those whose lives we touch, even briefly. And, I believe, strongly, that happiness and meaning are not attained by reaching a goal or a destination, but rather, during the spiral of the journey.

Forever Friendships

Sometimes forever friendships emerge from a single event, a tatter of time.

In 1979, I returned to Williamsburg from Roanoke, VA, newly single with two children to raise alone. Steven was nine. Shannon was barely five. Finding a job was a minor detail compared to finding a place to live. At that time, landlords didn't want to rent to single women. I had to ask the husband of a friend to sign for me. I was lucky to find a nice house in a quiet, family neighborhood with a yard and lots of trees. I wanted the transition to be as easy as possible for the kids, so they stayed with my mom while I moved, unpacked, and decorated their rooms exactly as they were in our previous house. The rental house was not new or as beautiful as the one we were forced to leave, but everything considered, I was proud of the finished product. The kids were just happy to be home with me and all their things.

I found an interesting job, working for Colonial Williamsburg's famed archeologist, Ivor Noel Hume. I lasted two weeks. When I asked to be transferred, I was told I lasted two weeks longer than the last secretary, who left the first day. I was transferred to Group Visits to be executive assistant to the director, Mary Ann Brendel. It was my lucky day. She trained and supervised the interpreters who escorted the school groups who came from all over the country to tour the historic area. Our office also booked those tours. It was a small, wonderfully loyal staff who took pride in their work. We turned out great interpreters. I immediately felt at home and Mary Ann was a wonderful boss. One of my first assignments was to apprentice for a week with each of the craftspeople. What better way to learn what they do, than to do it. I carved a violin front with the Musical Instrument Maker. I poured and polished pewter spoons with the Silversmith. I learned to set type by hand on an 19th century printing press. I watched powdered wigs being made and had a fun week in the costume department as genius seamstresses created elegant ball gowns and satin knee breeches. It was the ultimate in craft adventure!

Meanwhile, Steven and Shannon were happy in their new school, made friends in the neighborhood, and occasionally, I got a child support check. Those stopped entirely after a few months, and I was unable to locate my ex. Eventually, I tracked him down in Arizona, but still, no checks. That would continue for years. Child support agencies would find him. Then he would disappear again. That's why I took on a second job with Mary Kay Cosmetics, working from home at night and on week-ends. I kept both jobs until I became a MK Sales Director and earned my first company car. I was sad to leave Group Visits and was forever grateful for the CW experience and the friends I made there.

Prior to moving to Roanoke because of my husband's job, we had lived in Williamsburg since 1963, so I had lots of friends to come back to when we returned three years later. But they were mostly couples. You can only endure being the third-wheel at dinner so many times. When my neighbor, Lori, mentioned a support group called Parents Without Partners, I was reluctant. I was shy. The thought of a whole room full of strangers was scary. Lori refused to give up, so finally, I went to a gathering. Turned out to be life-changing.

Unlike other singles groups, this one was family-oriented with picnics and game nights along with the adult activities. Steven and Shannon met other kids from divorced families, plus had lots of father figures to learn from and have fun with. My PWP friends became my second family. I had girlfriends again. We baby-sat for each other, shopped together. I even dated a couple of nice guys who are still my dear friends today. I got involved in administration of our local chapter, and became the party planner-yes, shy me! Looking back, that was such a serendipitous time in my life-just *a tatter of time*-but it changed everything. It helped my kids to feel normal again, to move past some of the pain and sadness of their father leaving them. It gave us fun things to do as a family.

The friendships begun there continued through the years. When Steven was a teenager, one of my PWP guy friends, was the person who took him to his first rock concert. Recently, he needed some advice regarding a new business he'd started. Another friend, stepped up to help. Parents Without Partners gave us a support system of amazing friends that we still have today. AND, the most serendipitous thing of all-I met my soulmate/husband, Don, on a blind date set up by a PWP girlfriend. That's the gift that just kept giving!

A Writing Life

I am a poet and author of four children's books, three memoirs, three books of poetry, an affirmation journal, a how-to book, and a travel book.

I grew up in the Appalachian Mountains of West Virginia, a coal miner's daughter. You can read about those early experiences in my memoir, *Daughter of the Mountains*. I married my high school sweetheart at nineteen. Seventeen years and two children later, the marriage ended, leaving me with a son, Steven, 9 and a daughter, Shannon, 4, to raise alone.

Writing has always been my way of coping with life' s challenges. As a single parent, I poured my joys and frustrations into journals that became poetry books, *Tapestry*; and *Walk with Me*. Children's stories became picture books, R*evolt of the Teacups; Buddy, the Bookworm*; and B*uddy and Ballerina Save the Library*, illustrated by my granddaughters, Adaline and Emma.

I met my soulmate/husband on a blind date. For twenty years, we camped and hiked our way through the U. S., Canada, and British Columbia. Don was a photographer, so we collaborated on travel stories, and I published a travel memoir, *Road Trip*, chronicling our adventures. One of those stories, about a mysterious encounter with hermit crabs in the British Virgin Islands, was published as a children's book, *Herman the Hermit Crab and the Mystery of the Big, Black, Shiny Thing*.

I kept a journal during the two years of the Covid pandemic, which became, *Twenty-four Months that Changed the World*. During those months, I also created an affirmation journal, called, *Begin Somewhere*. Recently, I decided to downsize from a large house to a townhome. Those challenges and misadventures became a how-to book, *The Move*. The stories in this book, *Been there, Done That…Happy Dance*, derived from blogs I wrote for my website.

    I believe our lives are built around words that not only tell the tales of where we' ve been, but carry us to the places we' d like to go next. Words continue to be my tools as I visualize and turn the pages of my life.

I Used To Think...

I used to think that acquisitions equaled happiness. I grew up in a small coal mining town in West Virginia. We didn't have indoor plumbing until I was in junior high school. When you have very little, things become very important. When I grew up, I acquired all the highly recommended things and people-a husband, two perfect children, a house in the suburbs, a station-wagon, and a dog. Unfortunately, instead of happiness, I was handed a divorce. I began life anew with a nine-year-old, a four-year-old, two jobs, and a return to college. The husband was gone, the house was sold, the dog ran away, but I knew I still had the important things-my sanity and my children, who, during those single-mom years, grew into responsible caring adults, who I not only love, but truly like and admire.

When a wonderful man came into our lives, there were lots more acquisitions as we built a new life together-a house in the country, full of books and art treasures from our twenty years of traveling. I reverted comfortably back to that equation of acquisitions equal happiness. I was certainly happy. So, it must be true. Then I lost my husband to cancer. I still had the house and all the things, but, of course, they didn't fill the hole. Out of that darkness came my personal truth. For me, it is moments that equal happiness-a magnificent sunset on a deserted white sand beach; the breath-taking view from the top of a mountain you just climbed; watching your children get married; holding your first grandchild-simple moments. Things go away, people leave us, but those moments, like videos, are with us forever, to be replayed when we need them. Miraculously, every morning we wake up with the option to create new ones.

Open A New Door

Each dawn opens a new door of opportunity…

    To mend a quarrel, believe in healing.

    Keep a promise, find time to show up.

    Examine your daily demands on others.

    Notice and protect the beauty of the earth.

    Listen, try to understand another's beliefs.

    Write a letter to a friend, encourage a child.

    Appreciate, be kind, laugh a little more.

    Release your fears, embrace your truth.

    Nurture your soul, worship your God.

    Hold onto hope, trust in possibilities.

    Celebrate the love in your life.

    Speak your love, again and again.

Each new day offers promise, growth.

The "O" Word

Part 6

Been There - Done That
Happy Dance!

Older Than Dirt

A friend sent me a quiz the other day with a list of things designed to determine whether I am older than dirt. The list provided a nostalgic stroll down memory lane.

- PARTYLINE TELEPHONES provided entertainment for the whole community when I was a teenager. There are no secrets in a small town, so if you wanted to get news out or spread a rumor, you just called one person. By the next day, it was everywhere. My girlfriend and I talked on the phone for hours every night, so it wasn't unusual for someone to pop in and request to use the phone. It was all very congenial.

- NEWSREELS BEFORE THE MOVIE gave us a big-screen taste of the world outside our little town-a world of wars, sports, and glamorous movie stars in fur coats. That was before fur became a dirty word. I was in my early teens when our first movie theatre opened. The debut movie was Love Me Tender, with Elvis Presley. I saw it four times and fell madly in love with The King. Still am!

- WASHTUB WRINGERS were a big step up for my mom. Previously, she would wash clothes in a big metal tub and wring everything out by hand. Then, she'd carry the clothes up the rock steps behind our house and hang them on the line, even in winter. I still remember her sitting by our pot-bellied stove at night, rubbing Vaseline into her red, chapped hands. The wringer washer was a miracle!

- HOME MILK DELIVERY IN GLASS BOTTLES was common in nearby towns. But our milk was delivered every morning in a metal bucket, foaming fresh and warm from my Aunt Kaye's cows. It became many things-butter that we churned in a wooden jar and sometimes, cottage cheese, aged in cheesecloth. Today's cottage cheese bears no resemblance to the small, tangy curds that were left after the milk soured and the whey was drained away.

- CANDY CIGARETTES were one of my favorite treats as a child. We'd pretend to smoke them, then crunch the thin, sweet sticks. We didn't know, of course, that real cigarettes were lethal. We would make the box last a long time because candy treats were rare, only for special occasions, like birthdays and Christmas. Recently, I wrote a story for my family newsletter about my first shopping adventure at the age of eight. I talked about buying penny candy for my little brother and me with my left-over Christmas shopping money-things like candy cigarettes, coconut slices, taffy, fruit chews and Dubble Bubble Gum. On Christmas morning, when I opened my present from my very clever son-in-law, I discovered a box, full of all those treats. He had tracked down every candy I had mentioned, even the Dubble Bubble Gum!

- TABLE-SIDE JUKE BOXES were usually found in dark, smoky, bar-like places. One exception was the small, family-run hot dog and hamburger joint across from my high school. We had an hour for lunch each day so my friends and I would dash across the street to grab a booth and order our chile/cheese dogs before the rush. We'd pool our left-over nickels and fight over which songs to choose on the jukebox, usually Elvis or the Everly Brothers.

In my senior year, during the last week of school, a bunch of us decided to skip school one afternoon and hang out there. This was a first for me. The juke box was blaring, people were dancing, when, suddenly, the front door opened and the principal was standing there, scowling. He lined us up and marched us back across the quiet, neighborhood street to his office, closed the door and said, "I considered letting you get by with a skip afternoon. I know it's your last week of school. But then, I thought about what a bad example that would set for the other students, especially since Cookie is student body president, Sharon is president of the Honor Society, and the rest of you are cheerleaders." Heads down, duly shamed, we crept back to class. Word spread quickly. By day's end, we were all heroes. I always wondered if Principal Hinkle realized his shaming plan had back-fired.

I continued to go down the oldness test list…Pea-shooters; Howdy Doody; 45 RPM records; 78 RPM records; 33 1/3 hi-fi records (all of which I still hoard in my record cabinet); metal ice trays with levers; blue flashbulbs; cork popguns; Studebakers; and TV test patterns that appeared after the last show ended at 11p.m., and were followed by the national anthem blaring against a fluttering flag background. The test pattern stayed on the screen until morning.

I remembered clearly, everything on the list. I also recalled a recent question from my young granddaughter. We were taking votes on a place for a quick lunch. "Gramma, what was your favorite fast-food place when you were my age?" She was shocked when I told her we had no such thing when I was growing up. We ate at home, whatever Mom chose to cook, and if we didn't like it, we had the option of sitting at the table until we did.

Oh my! I really am older than dirt.

Body Betrayal

If you could change something about yourself or your world, what would it be? The things that come to my mind are money, relationships, or world peace. Granted, I would love to win the lottery and use that money to build homeless shelters, pay off my kids' student loans and mortgages, send my grandchildren to college, debt-free. Oh, happy day! And it might be nice to be swept off my feet by a handsome millionaire who wanted me to travel the world with him. That would be hard to pass up. As I was contemplating world peace, it seemed so far beyond reach, my mind took me away from altruism altogether, and in a totally different direction.

Selfishly, what I would really like is my 35-year-old body back. I'd even settle for my 45-year-old body. I know, it's a pipe-dream but just picture this…

- I could fit into all those clothes in the back of the closet that I've been saving for that someday when I am once again a size 8.

- I could go to my class reunion and be the envy of all those beautiful people I always envied. Such sweet revenge!

- I could return to climbing mountains and hiking in rain forests without stopping every fifteen minutes to rest my aching back. Actually, I would be happy to just hike the mile around my neighborhood, pain-free.

- All those bucks I'm handing over to the chiropractor could pay for a luxurious spa vacation, complete with massages and make-overs in some romantic city, maybe Rome.

- I could wear cute shoes again instead of those sensible, stabilizing, incredibly ugly ones.

- Let's not forget those 35-year-old eyes that could safely drive at night, to plays and concerts and wee-hour parties.

You get the picture. I don't mind getting older. It's all the body betrayal that goes along with it. I deserve better. I ate healthy foods. I avoided alcohol and cigarettes. I exercised and got those recommended eight hours of shut-eye a night. I read health magazines, took my vitamins, and maintained a positive outlook on life. The positive outlook is still there, though a bit blurred by cataracts and slowed down by arthritis. But I'm hanging in there, waiting impatiently for the first complete body transplant.

WHEN IS OLD?

By: Steven Dorsey

As I begin this day, my 52nd birthday, I can't help but think…what happens when you can't fully put Humpty Dumpty back together again? That's the dilemma I've faced over the last few years. There are days when my head tells me I'm still 20, but my body says, "Nope, not today". How do you fight Father Time when it seems the battery is always running down in your watch? Come sit around the campfire, kiddies. I will tell you how I got to this point.

Now don't go thinking that I have not looked in a mirror and noticed that I have more hair on my arms than on my head. Painful to acknowledge, but true. I think the first time this whole age thing became real was about three years ago when I went to get a new pair of contact lenses. I have worn contacts forever, but about three years ago I needed a new pair and was told I might want to think about getting bifocal contacts. Wait? What? As I looked around the room to see who my doctor was talking to, she then explained, at a certain age your eyes change. Huh? A certain age? Me? Not on your life. Three years later, I still can't find a pair of contact lenses that will work for me. And yes, it's because my eyes have changed. I am officially "that certain age" plus a couple.

That's ok though, isn't it? Things change. I still play video games with the kids, listen to the same music I listened to when I was 20, so I can't be old, can I? Age has a way of creeping up and smacking you on the back of the head when you're not looking. My kids have slowly started overtaking me in the speed department. I can still muscle them around on the basketball court, but my metabolism has slowed to a turtle's pace, and my once youthful figure has taken on more of a bowling pin appearance.

At the height of the pandemic, my family and I went on a picnic to a local park, and played baseball after we ate. My oldest daughter hit a mean line drive right up the middle. I swear it slowed down long enough for me to watch it bounce off my shin and feel the pain ripple through my body. I don't remember what words came out of my mouth as I collapsed into a screaming heap, but I doubt they were in any of the kids' school dictionaries. Another thing you find out when you get older is your body does not heal on demand. It doesn't even take requests. To this day, I still have a knot on my shin that will not go away. It's been over a year.

At the end of the baseball season, my son's coach surprised the kids with a parents-versus-kids kickball game. I love kickball. Except that night, I didn't kick well (in my defense, the parents had to use their less dominant foot-no really, we did.) I was slower than every little kid on the field. So much so, the coach encouraged me to run fast, like my son. While I'm not proud of my performance that day, I was at least happy he acknowledged Zachary was running much faster this season. So that's a win, right?

What's the moral of the story? Old is certainly a state of mind unless you're playing kickball with a bunch of 2nd and 3rd graders. Then your oldness is on full display. The music that was cool when I was 20 is now old man music. I have to take my glasses off and hold my Nintendo Switch up to my face to play video games. Hair-cuts only take about five minutes, maybe ten if you include trying to book the next one. Do I feel old? There are certainly days when getting out of bed hurts. And, there are days I feel like the old man yelling, "Back in my day….".

You know what though? I still listen to the Beatles and R.E.M., plus whatever new music piques my interest. I even have Spotify on my phone. I'll keep playing video games. I'll continue to run slower than my kids. I'll also continue to threaten to play my guitar like Tommy Emmanuel, (though that's less and less likely). I'll never be 20. That's perfectly fine. I'm comfortable in my fifty-two-year-old skin. Although I am growing weary of taking my glasses off to read tiny print. That drives me nuts. Don't forget…whatever your age, eat your dessert first!

Aging with Friends

Becky has vertigo, now needs a cane.
Can't find a cause and the cures are inane.

Kay broke her hip and is now in rehab.
Pat goes to Mayo in March for new labs.

Janie is late for important meetings,
plus, can't recall if she's the one leading.

Judy just fell and has broken her arm.
She keeps insisting, "I'm fine. There's no harm."

Peggy's back problems were caused by a dog,
who dragged her along, on his morning jog.

Debi's about to replace both her knees.
Marilyn's breathing is tinged with a wheeze.

Ann has decided she can't drive at night.
We'll eat early dinner, while it's still light.

Our lunch conversation centers around
competent doctors someone has just found.

Now when the phone rings, I grab keys and purse,
wait to see which of my friends needs a nurse.

We've been through divorces, babies and wakes,
there for each other, whatever it takes.

Embracing Oldness

I celebrated my 81st birthday this week. I'm a little sad to be 81, but also happy that I reached that new plateau. Many of my friends weren't so fortunate. I've decided the worst part of getting older is not the gray hair or aching back. It's losing my friends-the people I went to school with, raised my children with, wandered through middle age with-the people who know me and have loved me anyway.

Who will I reminisce with, when those old friends are gone? I remember my mother lamenting losing her girlfriends. At the time, I sympathized, but I didn't truly understand until it started happening to me. Out of habit, I picked up the phone last night to call my friend, Jenny. We've been friends for over forty years and always chatted on the week-ends. I teared-up as it hit me all over again that she had died of a sudden heart attack two weeks ago.

I moved recently, which necessitated a lot of purging. An old trunk yielded photos, letters, and keepsakes, going all the way back to my school days. Why do we keep those things from so long ago? I think it's because it connects us to our roots, validates who we are, or were. As I looked at those young faces, some now nameless, I wondered what had happened to them. Did they grow up to marry and have kids of their own like me? Were they successful in their lives? Were they happy?

So many stories whose endings I can never know. I will have to be content with the memories of that time and place and let the endings go. As I placed those remnants of youth into the recycle bin, I knew I didn't need the stuff to keep the memories alive.

Embracing oldness is not just a matter of accepting my own elder status, but also that of my friends. I spent some time on the phone yesterday with Janie, my friend of fifty+ years. We were single parents together, struggling to work, raise kids, stay sane. Laughter saved us. It still does. Janie lives in the shadowy world of short-term memory disease. She's able to continue to live on her own, but had to give up driving. Her early memories are still there, so she recalls our connection, and our history. But when I hang up the phone from talking with her, she won't remember later in the day that I called.

She is remarkedly cheerful, living completely in the moment, enjoying whatever that moment brings, before it's gone. At first, I felt sad for her until I realized she delights in things the rest of us take for granted or might not notice-a bird on the window sill, daffodils coming up in her little garden space, the sun on her face when she sits on her porch. Tomorrow, those same experiences will be new to her again. Each day is a fresh start, and she's happy.

When I was in my late twenties, I became part of a Sweet Adeline barbershop chorus. It was the one thing in my life that was just for me, a break from being a stay-at-home mom with a two-year-old. The women in that group became my extended family. Janie was one of them. Jeannie was another. (I know, what's with all the J's?) We have remained best friends for over fifty years. We used to laugh about growing old together. We fantasized about getting a big house and singing our way through our senior years.

It was a good plan, but reality, unfortunately, always intervenes. Jeannie now lives in Arizona. She and her husband, Jim, came to Williamsburg for a visit a couple of months ago. Janie joined us for a Sweet Adeline reunion. Jeannie founded the barbershop chorus. She was one of the most energetic people I'd ever known, always smiling, buzzing around much too fast in her sports car, or flying off somewhere with Jim in their small plane. She was this tiny, fearless blonde-pilot, skydiver-game to try anything. Over the years, health issues and worsening eye disease put an end to her flying and driving. I visited her in Arizona several times. I was amazed at how well she had adapted as the eye problems worsened and darkness began to close in. She never complained. She maintained her love of music, going to concerts and plays as she always had.

The Williamsburg visit was fun, with lots of jokes about our collective oldness challenges. Janie asked Jim to take a photo of us, so she would be able to remember the visit. Jeannie laughingly demanded it be enlarged enough that she could "kind of" see it. I loved the fact that no one took themselves or their problems very seriously. We all felt as if we were thirty again.

I am fortunate to have lots of friends who have been in my life for many years. I treasure those people. We see each other and like each other for the persons we've always been. When I'm with them, I still feel thirty or forty or fifty or whatever age we were when the friendship began. Our gray hair, the canes, the sensible shoes are surface things, like costumes for a play. It is what it is. Beneath those surface changes, we still feel young at heart. We accept each other's frailties, embrace our limitations, and keep on, keepin' on. Instead of goodbyes, we end our visits with hugs and our mantra, "Que sera, sera," Whatever will be, will be.

Oh, Those Birthdays!

Hickory, dickory, dock.
We can't turn back the clock.
No point worrying about our age.
Growing older is just a stage.

Now we'll complain about poor memory,
while soaking our feet and drinking green tea.
We'll go out shopping to buy a new hat,
look in the mirror and ask, "Who is that?"

We'll dine out early to get home by dark,
and never attempt to parallel park.
We'll ban healthy snacks as simply the worst,
and solemnly swear to eat dessert first.

The Soundtrack Of My Life

Days dissolve into months, months into years.
Years march down the rabbit hole into oblivion.
Memories keep lost loved ones alive, remind us of
adventures that brought us joy or sometimes, pain.

But nothing stirs our emotions and carries us back
in time like music-the soundtrack of our lives. I love
40's music because it brings back images of scratched
78's spinning on my dad's old console record player.

I recall my grandma tapping her feet and clapping her
hands to a rousing chorus of, "That Old Time Religion."
Chords from those songs bring faces and voices to
life again better than any photograph album could.

My *fifty-something children* appreciate 50's and
60's music because I played it constantly when they
were little. Their dad and I jitterbugged to *Blue Suede
Shoes*. The Everly Brothers sang them to sleep.

I have been stitched together by the drums and flutes of
powwows; the commanding tones of church choirs; the
acapella of barbershop choruses; mellow jazz saxophones;
and the haunting harmonies of the Moody Blues.

Music therapy is being used more-and-more to pull
Alzheimer's patients from the shadows back into the
light for brief moments. If I ever slip into that sad place,
just play some Elvis, any Elvis, and I'll back!

My Love/Hate Relationship With Aging

My hair now is graying. My knees creak and crack.
My back aches in rain storms. I can't eat Big Macs.

I cannot climb mountains. My kayak is gone.
I won't wear a swimsuit. I don't mow the lawn.

Some things, however, are freeing and fun.
There's more time to travel, just chasing the sun.

I write in my pjs, curled up by the fire,
while housework gets done, by someone I hire.

I say no without guilt, to meetings and clubs.
They now run without me, while I get back rubs.

On bright, sunny mornings, I wake up at nine,
and thank the Great Spirit, I still have my mind!

Downsizing Can Bring You Joy

What eighty-year-old woman wakes up on a sunny day in May and decides to change her entire life? One who is tired of a big house in the woods that demands constant attention and maintenance; deer that devour flowers and shrubs; rabbits that eat everything left by the deer; and a neighbor's chickens who poop on her sidewalks. That, by-the-way, was the last straw. It was time to abandon ship! But how do you downsize from a 3,100 sq. ft. house, a two-car garage and four large storage buildings–all overflowing with stuff collected over a lifetime of travels, children, moves, and just living-into a townhome?

How do you decide what to keep and what must go? How do you find homes for cherished furniture and belongings that won't fit into the new place? Do you keep your high school yearbooks? What about those scrapbooks full of memories of your children's childhoods? Do you really need a drawer of Tupperware? How do you scale down three walls of books? What do you do with a twenty-year collection of Native American art items? And on and on…

I survived all that to emerge from a jumble of long-lost items and long-forgotten memories, to a place of lightness and freedom that comes from letting go of things and emotional baggage, and moving on, into a brand-new life. To celebrate, I wrote a book about it, called, *The Move*. I recommend it, promise you'll enjoy the ride, with all the struggles and laughter along the way. You'll learn a lot about downsizing, and maybe, a little about yourself.

Eighty-Two...Who Knew?

Who knew...

- Going gray could be so freeing!
- Gray hair and a cane would inspire people to offer to unload my grocery cart.
- My new look would prompt friends to say, "Who is that foxy lady?"
- Shrinking comes with aging. That's so unfair-old AND short?
- Grocery shopping on Senior Day gives you savings to buy earrings.
- You never have too many earrings.
- Staying in your pajamas on a week-day can be luxurious.
- Sensible shoes are this year's senior rage.
- Downsizing is liberating. Your stuff can be happy someplace else.
- You could wake up one morning and decide to fly to Hawaii. Why not?
- Watching Dr. Odyssey is more fun than real life petri-dish cruises.
- One can resign from cooking and enjoy culinary delights anytime with Door Dash.
- It is sometimes necessary to explain to the uninformed, "Just because I'm a grand dame, I am not stupid, incapable of learning new things, OR finished!"

Eighty-two...who knew it could be delightful!

My Soap Box

Part 7

Been There - Done That
Happy Dance!

Technology And Me

It all started when my three-year-old printer went down. I called Staples to complain and was told flatly and unemotionally, "Yeah, they're only built to last a couple of years. If you got three, you're lucky." I did not feel lucky as I plunked down money, then tried to figure out how to hook up and use the new machine.

Next, the DVR malfunctioned, which necessitated a visit to the Cox office with another machine to install and master. The mastering took a couple of days. I celebrated with popcorn and a freshly taped movie.

Strike three happened a few days later when the cable AND the internet went down on the evening I'd planned to watch the Golden Globes. It was AWOL the rest of the night. As I'm writing this, I'm realizing maybe I'm a little too attached to my television, which is depressing. I spent a quiet evening reading a book and cleaning my bathroom. I know, I know. I really should get a social life.

Sunday, I had planned to write poetry. Rarely, do I have a whole day for this thing I love so much-venting at the computer, in meter and rhyme. Grumpy Father Fate said, "I don't think so," and senselessly murdered my computer. All the king's horses and my best online computer Obi One couldn't put Humpty Computer back together again. At this writing, Bob is draped in black, waiting for Obi One to arrive, carry him away, and attempt to breathe life back into him. Yes, I do realize naming my computer is a little weird, but I thought if I named him and talked sweetly to him, he might live longer. Apparently not. He's barely three.

All of this makes me long for those childhood days, when the television repairman came with his suitcase full of glass tubes, took the back off the television, and tried tube after tube till he found the right one, bringing black and white magic back into our lives. Those were the days when workmanship was a given, repairmen became lifelong friends, and we weren't a throw-away society.

Computer Warfare

I have a computer named Bob,
who sometimes sits down on the job.
I warned him today.
He will have to pay.
Tomorrow he meets the Geek Squad.

Teachers Deserve More Money and More Respect!!!!

As teachers close their classrooms for the year, pile their belongings and weary bodies into cars and head home, let's hope it's a summer of rest and relaxation they so richly deserve, not a second job. Teachers across the country have marched and carried signs this year, trying to create awareness of their very real needs for higher pay and better treatment. I hope they get both.

Each of us probably had at least one teacher who inspired us, believed in us when we didn't believe in ourselves. I had a high school English teacher who was the first person to tell me she thought I had a talent for writing. She wrote those words on one of my essays. I kept that faded piece of paper for years. Sometimes, it takes only one person believing, to send us on our way to achieving our dreams.

Teachers, if you get depressed about your working conditions, it could be worse.

Rules For Teachers…1872

1. Teachers will fill lamps, clean chimneys each day. Each teacher will bring a bucket of water and a scuttle of coal for the day's session.

2. Make your pens carefully. You may whittle nibs to the taste of each pupil.

3. Men teachers may take one evening each week for courting purposes or two evenings a week if they go to church regularly.

4. After ten hours in school, teachers may spend the remaining time reading the Bible or other good books.

5. Women teachers who marry or engage in unseemly conduct will be dismissed.

6. Every teacher should lay aside from each pay a goodly sum of his earnings for his benefit during his declining years so he will not become a burden to society.

7. Any teacher who smokes or uses liquor will be dismissed.

8. Any teacher who frequents pool halls, or gets shaved in a barbershop will give good reason to suspect his worth, intention, integrity, and honesty.

9. The teacher who performs his labor faithfully and without fault for five years will be given an increase of twenty-five cents per week in his pay, providing the Board of Education approves.

Indigenous Peoples' Day

Today, most people know that the legacy and achievements of the explorer, Christopher Columbus, who the nation once dutifully celebrated, depict a false narrative, honoring a man who initiated the colonization of the peoples indigenous to the Americas. Native people had lived in these lands for thousands of years before European contact.

I wonder if most people realize just how far-reaching the impact of Columbus, the pirate, and his voyages truly were. Within a century of European arrival, entire communities had begun to disappear. Natives were killed. They were enslaved. They died of disease. They were brutally exploited for their land and belongings.

We cannot go back in time and change the attitudes of colonists and conquerors of a time now far away-men who thought whatever they discovered was theirs to take. But we can act in a way that shows we will no longer celebrate the exploitation of one people by another.

Many cities, counties, and universities have begun celebrating Indigenous Peoples' Day or Native American Day, instead of Columbus Day. It is a way of acknowledging the truth about the past, so we can make positive changes in the present. It is honoring the achievements of indigenous peoples whose social, cultural, artistic, musical, scholarly, and literary accomplishments have contributed so much to our country.

It is especially appropriate for Virginians. On October 3, 2018, members of seven Virginia tribes gathered to celebrate being formally recognized by the federal government. They gathered at Werowocomoco, in Gloucester County, on land once occupied by their ancestors. It's been a long time coming. The Pamunkey, Chickahominy, Chickahominy Eastern Division, Monacan, Nansemond, Rappahannock, and Upper Mattaponi fought for federal recognition for decades. The designation guaranteed the tribes sovereignty to decide their own destiny. It restored to them rights that were stolen generations ago.

Rappahannock Chief, Anne Richardson voiced the feelings of tribal members, "This is liberty for us. This is justice for us. We're finally seeing the promises that are inherent in our constitution that we've been left out of all these years."

The World Needs A Talking Stick

I am a talking stick. I was carved from a piece of cedar, chosen for my interesting shape, the grain and strength of my wood. I was carried to a drying building, where I was allowed to season for several months. Then, a talented carver whittled and sanded me into a talking stick.

I am descended from a Native American tradition. I have helped to mediate territorial disputes, avoiding wars. The elder of a tribe or village would hold the talking stick and begin a discussion. When he was finished, he would pass it to the next person and the next, until everyone who wished to speak had done so. Whoever held the talking stick held the power of words. Everyone else had to remain silent and listen.

This allowed quiet members of a group to speak their truth too. It helped to create equality and respect for other opinions. Holding it provided uninterrupted time to collect thoughts. In those quiet moments, the speaker might discover feelings or ideas they had not acknowledged or shared. The talking stick is a powerful reminder of the validity of other points of view.

We can find answers to difficult questions through listening. We learn that life has many options, many paths. If we allow ourselves to be guided by the wisdom of others through the talking stick, we may be given an opportunity to grow through alternative routes. Perhaps it's time for our government leaders to adopt the empowerment of the talking stick, and start listening to each other. On a broader scale, the United Nations could benefit from a very LARGE talking stick.

We could create a new motto, "Talk softly and carry a carved stick." Imagine a world where we listen to each other. Our angry, ready-to-explode planet has never needed a talking stick more.

Acceptance can Make our World a Better Place

I mmigrants are being removed from our country daily. Black parents are forced to have *the talk* with their teenagers for fear they are at risk from police officers.

White Supremacists march with upraised fists and chant, "Jews will not replace us."

LGBTQ individuals are being barred from serving in our military and face daily discrimination.

We are not born with prejudices. Watch little kids play together. They might fight over toys, but they don't fight over the color of their skins. At what age does the hatred creep in? Why?

There were no black people in the small town where I grew up, but we had lots of Italians. My dad hated them. He would say, over and over, "Those S. O. B.'s came over here and took our jobs!" He was a coal miner and felt threatened because the desperate refugees would work for less money. Two of my best friends in high school were Italian. I wasn't allowed to invite them to our home. I also couldn't go to theirs. That was in the 50's. Today, we hear the same thing about Latinos taking our jobs. Truth is, they take jobs nobody else wants.

Why are we threatened by people whose skin color, country of origin, or religious beliefs are different from ours? How can we overcome the fear and hatred?

Perhaps dialogue, honest dialogue, could begin the journey. Talking to each other would reveal the things we have in common-children, jobs, money worries. It should be harder to hate someone you have taken the time to get to know. Knowledge should wipe out the stereotypes we have in our minds. It all sounds so simple. So why haven't we done it? Some people have and do, but not enough people.

Also, it's much more difficult to pursue a path of acceptance and unconditional love when our leaders spew fear of anyone different from us. In many ways, citizens are like children, looking to our leaders to be parent figures, role models. When those leaders are lacking in empathy and acceptance, they attract followers who also have no moral guide star. Chaos ensues. I fear our natural inclination is to hide in our little corner of the world, where we feel safe, and take the stance, "That's not my problem. Let someone else fight that battle." However, the battle must start with each of us.

When was the last time you attended a church service different from your own? Have you ever invited an exchange student into your home, even for a holiday, when they were far from family? Do you attend political debates to learn about the values and beliefs of the people you are choosing to run our country? Have you ever sought out a military family whose husband or wife is off in a foreign land, fighting for your safety, and offered support? Do you know or care why we are at war in those lands? Do you defend immigrants' rights to seek refuge here? Do you remind yourself that your ancestors were probably refugees too? We all are, unless we're descended from Native Americans. Why are today's immigrants any less worthy of sanctuary than our ancestors?

Ignorance too often breeds hatred. It is the enemy of acceptance. Without acceptance of those different from ourselves, there can be no peace, not in our hearts, on our streets, or in the world.

GAY PRIDE
by my forever friend, Carlton Hardy

GAY PRIDE MONTH... A month when parades and festivals across America celebrate the diversity that is the LGBTQ+ community, the contributions made, and the ongoing struggle for equality in the eyes of the law, and the community-at-large of friends, family, neighbors, co-workers. A celebration standing on the shoulders of those who grew up in the 1950s, 1960s, 1970s, 1980s, 1990s, etc. A celebration standing on the shoulders of those who survived the McCarthy era and the Red Menace, who survived the Hollywood witch hunts, the Anita Bryants, Aids, "don't ask-don't tell," and now the hatred, discrimination, and scapegoating of ethnic, cultural, and racial minorities in the guise of Christian Nationalism and fascism. When conservative Christians weaponize the Bible to justify xenophobic policy while ignoring Christ's teachings, it ceases to be biblical theology and becomes political idolatry.

I did not grow up as myself. I grew up playing a version of myself that sacrificed authenticity to minimize humiliation and prejudice. While I was abysmal at playing sports, I tried desperately to fit in. I learned during eleventh grade, if you threw yourself into group tasks (building the homecoming float, decorating for the Ring Dance, etc.) you could achieve a level of acceptance. I believed my worth was a function of what I did, and through those works, I could achieve a level of acceptance and recognition. The massive task of my adult life-which spans more than half a century-has been to unravel which parts of myself are truly me and which parts were created for self-preservation. I have been told it's not what you do that is of value, it is who you are.

Who am I? I am. Two small words. The definition has taken over a half century to find. I am a human being who is spiritual and creative. I am a human who happens to be Caucasian and male with certain learning disabilities balanced with proportionate compensations. I am a human who worked for a paycheck for over 53 years. I am a human who enjoys being retired. I am my hobbies, my affiliations, my sexuality, my biological family, my network, my extended "family" of friends. I am one who tries to brighten my little corner of the universe. I am one who tries to bring joy to others. I am one who believes you should help others whenever, wherever, and however you can. I am my interests, my experiences, my education, my failures, my successes, my values, things I'm good at, things I'm not good at, and my core values and beliefs. I am passionate about music and how music brings a richness and fullness to life, especially the King of instruments, the organ, and men's choral music. I am my fears-roller coasters, drugs, heights, being robbed, being in a mass shooting, a global war, outliving my money, dying alone.

I also happen to be homosexual. It was not a conscious decision. I did not at any time make a conscious choice to be gay. To be gay or not to be gay? Do I have a choice? Can I awaken tomorrow and simply decide, "I'm going straight?" I think not. The song, "I Am What I Am," from the production, *La Cage aux Follies*, tells us life is not worth a damn unless we can proclaim, I am what I am.

I did not wake up one day and decide, "Now I'm going to be gay." It was a gradual process. I cannot look back and say I've known I was gay since I was ten, or twelve, or fifteen. As I look back, I see that maybe I should have known, but I also see that I lacked the vocabulary to describe and discuss my feelings. I grew up in a small town with one elementary school and one high school. I also did not have anyone with whom to talk, so the lack of language didn't matter. It was not until I was thirty-five years old that I knew officially that I was gay. I did not have to struggle with this realization as it seemed a quite natural and normal process of self-acceptance.

Forty-six years have passed since that realization. I have now joined the "gay and gray" generation. I am proud of who I am. I am proud of the professional contributions I made during my career in education, distance learning, and writing Department of Defense policy. I am proud of the contributions I made in the world of business through the Virginia Peninsula Chamber of Commerce (VPCC) and the Hampton Roads Business OutReach (HRBOR). I am proud of my contributions to the world of arts and culture at the local, regional, and state level as a member of The Cultural Alliance of Greater Hampton Roads. I am proud to have been called an important arts contributor by Veer Magazine. I am proud to be remembered as the Father of the Virginians for the Arts license plate. I am proud of my contributions to regional transportation as a member and Vice Chair of the Planning District's Community Advisory Committee.

I am proud of my religious life and the contributions made to both my local congregation (a concert series and annual organ concert), and at the state level (creator and facilitator of the annual Serving Boldly Award for lay leadership). I am proud of my Equality Virginia Legend Award- That Others May Follow Your Light. I am proud to have mentored many up-and-coming LGBTQ+ leaders of tomorrow, for they will spread good works even further. They will work in the light rather than the shadows.

Now in my eighth decade, I acknowledge, I am bruised, but I am also brave. I now march to the beat of my own drum. I am who I was always meant to be. I owe no apologies. I am me.

COLORS OF OUR LIVES

Colors open memory windows for me. Some inspire feelings of pride. Others evoke images of family members, long gone. Some colors seem to have a soul.

PINK has dominated my life for over forty years-in my wardrobe, the color of my cars, and the products that have provided my livelihood. When I see pink, I am reminded of my mentor, Mary Kay Ash, whose company mission for sixty years has been to enrich women's lives. When I joined the company, I was presented with a long-stemmed pink rose and told, "We come into this business as tight, little rosebuds. As we learn and grow, we shed our fears and blossom into full-blown roses, capable of reaching out and helping others achieve their dreams." Mary Kay pink has taken me to amazing places, introduced me to talented, capable women, and gifted me with the joy of teaching and guiding hundreds of other amazing women. PINK, for me, represents strength, compassion, and unlimited opportunity.

GREEN is the color of new life, adventure. Green is the dampness of rain forests, the richness of emerald canopy overhead, spongy moss beneath my feet. Green is mountains to climb; unlimited vistas waiting at the end of the journey; exhilaration as tired muscles push through final steps to the top. Green is also the color of new life, as spring buds awaken from winter's sleep. GREEN is the color of renewal and hope.

BLACK is the color of coal that has hollowed out the mountains of Appalachia, and hollowed out the lives of the men who mine it. Black was the color of soot that imbedded itself into my Dad's skin and lungs, stealing his life when he was barely sixty. BLACK is the color of greed, environmental destruction, and death.

PURPLE is my favorite color. I have always felt it has a soul. The color, red, is powerful, blue is soothing, yellow is cheerful. But when you look at purple, it stares back at you with the wisdom of the ages. Purple clothed pharaohs, emperors and kings, during life and the afterlife. Amethyst stones were sacred, worn only by those thought to be gods. In ancient lands, purple saw birth and death, famine and plenty, cruelty, and compassion, through ions of man's struggles. The color PURPLE has a soul.

WE, THE PEOPLE

Webster's Dictionary defines the word, people as,
"Any group, community, tribe, to which one belongs."
By that definition, there are human people, tree people,
animal people, and numerous varieties of plant people.

Scientists now tell us that plants talk to each other,
reacting in tandem to weather warnings, dangers.
Trees communicate through their roots, strengthening
baby trees and weaker members of their community.

Dogs protect their owners, but also, other animals.
My friend has two dogs. One is blind. The seeing dog
escorts his friend around the yard, protecting him
from the coyote predators who search out the weak.

Websites are full of adorable pictures of mother ducks
escorting a line of babies across a busy city street;
kittens curled up with horses many times their size;
massive elephants mourning for days beside their dead.

If nature's people instinctively know the importance of
unity for survival, where, in the evolutionary chain did
humans lose or choose to ignore that essential truth?
More importantly, what can we can do to restore it?

It seems too late to stop humans from killing humans.
Is it also too late to keep humans from destroying the
tree people, the animal people, and the plant people?
Are there enough moments left to save Mother Earth?

The Rescuers

(Dedicated to all the fearless social workers)

They march across report pages…
young, old, brown, black, white, all sharing one commonality.
They have been abused by husbands, wives, parents, lovers.

When the physical and psychological pain becomes too great,
where do they turn? Not to the police, or to families, friends.
They pour their hearts out to strangers-social workers,
who ask questions, fill out piles of forms, fight for them in the
courts, and most importantly, listen and care.

Sometimes they care so much, they carry the concern for those
clients home with them, disturbing sleep and affecting health.
They are not in their jobs for the money. Salaries are sadly low.
They're also not there for recognition, although a message from
a grateful client saying, "You saved my life," shines up their day.

To all those selfless makers of miracles, ask yourself…
How many women or men did you rescue from hell this week?
How many children sleep safe and warm because of you?
How many homeless have shelter and food due to your efforts?

Remember all those things on the days when it seems that
society has lost its humanity, or the days when you are being
criticized for simply trying to do your job. There are multitudes
of people out there who know, and owe their lives and safety to you.

All you rescuers, may you sleep peacefully tonight and every night.

Woman, the Change Maker

I fed and clothed my tribe, curing buffalo hides
and drying meat over smoldering fires.

I civilized the Jamestown Colony in Virginia,
bringing family life to a new, unexplored territory.

I spoke for women in the Salem Witch Trials,
weeping as they were burned at the stake.

I fought for women's voices to be heard,
as far back as the Declaration of Independence.

I guided Lewis and Clark on their explorations of the West.
I braved covered-wagon journeys to settle the wilderness.

I was arrested for opening the first birth control clinic.
I still struggle for a woman's right to control her own body.

I went to war alongside my brothers.
I fought, I healed, and I died.

I infiltrated Congress and the Supreme Court,
bringing fair judgement and compassionate ideas.

I flew into space, exploring the final frontier,
bringing back information to guide future expeditions.

I was awarded the Nobel Peace Prize,
as the battle for education and human rights goes on.

I am resilient and courageous, charming, and cunning.
I am woman-the Change Maker.

The Other Ten Commandments

1. Thou shall not worry, for worry is the most unproductive of all human activities.

2. Thou shall not be fearful, for most of the things we fear never come to pass.

3. Thou shall not cross bridges before coming to them, for no one has yet succeeded in accomplishing this.

4. Thou shall face each problem as it comes. You can only handle one at a time anyway.

5. Thou shall not take problems to bed with you, for they make very poor bedfellows.

6. Thou shall not borrow other people's problems. They can better care for them.

7. Thou shall not try to relive yesterday, for, good or ill, it is gone forever.

8. Thou shall be a good listener, for only when you listen, do you hear ideas different from your own and grow in knowledge and acceptance.

9. Thou shall not become bogged down by frustration, for 90% of it is rooted in self-pity and will only interfere with positive action.

10. Thou shall count thy blessings, never overlooking the small ones, for a lot of small blessings add up to a big one.

BONUS COMMANDMENT…Thou shall love unconditionally.

Journey to the Pandemic

Part 8

Been There - Done That
Happy Dance!

Journey To The Pandemic, A Day At A Time, Feb. 20, 2019-Feb. 20, 2020

(Come along with me through my 76th birthday year as we keep on, keepin' on, a day at a time.)

FEBRUARY

FEB. 20, 2019: I am seventy-six today. How did that happen?

FEB. 21, 2019: Birthday cards pouring in. Still giggling at the sympathy card.

FEB. 22, 2019: My brother has been hospitalized for weeks. Makes my heart hurt.

FEB. 23, 2019: My granddad, a carpenter, was born on this day in 1894. He helped me purchase my first "single Mom" home.

FEB. 24, 2019: Saw a turtle snoozing in the tall grass. Do you think turtles dream?

FEB. 25, 2019: Some leaders are born women. They are now running for president.

FEB. 26, 2019: My granddaughter got braces. She's excited she looks like her friends.

FEB. 27, 2019: The robins are back. Who told them it was time to return?

FEB. 28, 2019: I have to deal with people today. Send chocolate!

MARCH

MARCH 1, 2019: I'm watching a mamma deer nuzzling her new fawn. Life renewing life.

MARCH 2, 2019: Today, I was amazing. Yesterday, I looked for my phone while talking on it.

MARCH 3, 2019: My friend's teenager says he could be a morning person if morning started at noon.

MARCH 4, 2019: Monday and the world's off to work, smiling on the outside, screaming on the inside.

MARCH 5, 2019: Spring happens in slow motion, buds opening before my eyes.

MARCH 6, 2019: Girls can lead, make smart decisions, say "no."

MARCH 7, 2019: Nothing changes, unless something changes.

MARCH 8, 2019: Six years ago, my husband departed this life for other realms. Wish he could send back texts.

MARCH 9, 2019: Don, If I had my life to live over, I would have found you sooner, so I could have loved you longer.

MARCH 10, 2019: Wrote a poem today about the aches and pains of aging. Each of my friends thought it was about her.

MARCH 11, 2019: If it's a Monday holiday, I declare it an "Add to Cart" day.

MARCH 12, 2019: I don't like camping-no electricity, no running water. It's paying money to live like I grew up in the 40's.

MARCH 13, 2019: My daughter's definition of "Flight of the Bumblebee" – flying around, throwing things into closets before guests arrive.

MARCH 14, 2019: My fall back for a rough day…could be worse…could be trying on bathing suits.

MARCH 15, 2019: Calories are tiny seamstresses who live in your closet and make your clothes smaller while you're sleeping.

MARCH 16, 2019: Fifty people were shot dead today because of hatred. Why do people want to destroy those different from themselves?

MARCH 17, 2019: My children grew up with Mister Rogers' Neighborhood. Today, we all wish we could move there.

MARCH 18, 2019: I have a friend who's a hoarder. He says it isn't hoarding if it's cool stuff.

MARCH 19, 2019: I don't mind getting older. I DO mind looking it.

MARCH 20, 2019: Every woman knows…it's better to arrive late, than ugly.

MARCH 21, 2019: My grandchildren live several states away. I've gotten really good at long-distance spoiling.

MARCH 22, 2019: Am I the only grandmother who thinks her grand-children are B&B-beautiful and brilliant?

MARCH 23, 2019: My favorite thing about Saturday is… EVERYTHING!

MARCH 24, 2019: I don't have gray hair. I have wisdom highlights.

MARCH 25, 2019: I had a list of things to do today. I did the first one-Get up.

MARCH 26, 2019: Can't believe it's almost the end of the month already. Do you ever feel as if more than one day sneaks by while you're sleeping?

MARCH 27, 2019: I woke up to frost this morning. The daffodils need sweaters.

MARCH 28, 2019: When I have to call my children about a computer problem, I remind them," I had to teach you how to use a spoon!"

MARCH 29, 2019: I'm having a very belated birthday lunch with a friend today. I think she should compensate by treating me to two desserts.

MARCH 30, 2019: I just realized I totally missed celebrating St. Patrick's Day. Think it will count if I wear green today?

MARCH 31, 2019: I won my 20th Mary Kay Cosmetics car today…one every two years for 39 years as a director. Let's hear it for lipstick!

APRIL

APRIL 1, 2019: I cleaned house today, top to bottom. April Fool! I just put things in less obvious places.

APRIL 2, 2019: We MUST keep talking about the caged children on the southern border. Who is going to reunite them with their grieving parents?

APRIL 3, 2019: Forsythia and daffodils bloom like sunshine around the yard. Pollen blooms like nuclear waste on the hood of my car.

APRIL 4, 2019: Saw a rabbit nibbling clover in the back yard. Left a basket out in case it's the Easter Bunny.

APRIL 5, 2019: I hate road work. Trucks run over me while I'm driving the 50-mile-an-hour speed limit.

APRIL 6, 2019: A friend texted today just to say hello. She must have known I needed a digital hug.

APRIL 7, 2019: My annual cardiology check-up was today. Paid money for someone to tell me my heart is still beating.

APRIL 8, 2019: Thought I saw a spider on the carpet-was a piece of yarn. It's dead yarn now.

APRIL 9, 2019: Sad news is…I went to the movies alone today. Good news is…I didn't have to share my pizza.

APRIL 10, 2019: Wish I could win the lottery. I'd pay off everybody's student loans.

APRIL 11, 2019: Saw an interesting t-shirt today. It said, "Go braless. It will pull the wrinkles out of your face."

APRIL 12, 2019: Why do we fertilize the lawn to make the grass grow, then complain about having to mow it?

APRIL 13, 2019: Went to lunch with friends today and fought over the tab. Nobody wanted to pay it.

APRIL 14, 2019: I miss my grandchildren who live out of state. Hugging the I Pad is just not the same.

APRIL 15, 2019: There are days when I wish I could retire. Then I remember, I've grown accustomed to food and a roof over my head.

APRIL 16, 2019: My grandson, age five, just got his first library card! In a blink, it will be a driver's license. Sometimes I hate that time flies.

APRIL 17, 2019: Today is "National Do No Housework Day". Wonder if we could campaign to make that a whole week.

APRIL 18, 2019: The birds woke me up this morning, chirping happiness. We should take lessons from them on our grumpy days.

APRIL 19: I sent my new book off to my publisher today. I have the same scared feeling I had when my baby went off to kindergarten.

APRIL 20: My mother passed away in April, six years ago. Wish she was here today to color Easter eggs with me.

APRIL 21: All the church parking lots were overflowing this morning at 11 a.m. All the local restaurants were overflowing at 12:05 with the Easter lunch bunch.

APRIL 22, 2019: Today is Earth Day. How many bags of rode-side trash did you pick up today?

APRIL 23, 2019: Why do you think people pollute the earth with trash? We must teach our children and grandchildren to respect their planetary home.

APRIL 24, 2019: Some "hit and run" person dented my car in a parking lot. Their carelessness cost $600 plus three days of rental car fees. Shame on you!

APRIL 25, 2019: Worked in the flower beds this morning. Did a week's worth of cardio after walking into a spider web.

APRIL 26, 2019: It's finally Friday! The first five days after a week-end are always the longest.

APRIL 27, 2019: Participated in a book show at Chesapeake Library. Our competition was a Pharrell Williams concert. Guess who won?

APRIL 28, 2019: My sense of direction leaves a lot to be desired. I sometimes wonder what happened to the lost people I tried to help.

APRIL 29, 2019: The lawn people AND the carpet cleaning people came today. If I had a chef and a housekeeper, I could pretend I live at Downton Abbey.

APRIL 30, 2019: The sun is shining, it's 75 degrees, the azaleas are in full bloom. I think I'll just be happy today.

MAY

MAY 1, 2019: I lost another friend this week. It's the worst part of growing older. I won't complain today about my aches and pains.

MAY 2, 2019: Our poetry group, the James City Poets, met today. I wrote a poem about pollen. Maybe poetry is "stuffy" after all.

MAY 3, 2019: I'm self-employed as a Mary Kay Cosmetics Sales Director. If you hear me talking to myself, I'm in a staff meeting.

MAY 4, 2019: I won three awards at the CNU Writer's Conference. A 1st in Poetry, a 2nd in Non-Fiction, and a 3rd in Juvenile Fiction. So happy!

MAY 5, 2019: I gave my daughter a t-shirt that says, "TOMORROW…a mythical land where everything I need to do is done." Amen!

MAY 6, 2019: A reminder for difficult times… Just when the caterpillar thought its world was over, it became a butterfly.

MAY 7, 2019: Saw a beautiful turtle today-orange markings on shell and head. He sat in the sun with me for a while, then crawled off on his journey to somewhere.

MAY 8, 2019: The zinnias I planted are up, waving their little green heads in the breeze. Nature's magic…brown seeds last week-pink, yellow, and orange blossoms soon.

MAY 9, 2019: My granddaughter, Emma, broke her wrist at school yesterday. Her sister, Adaline, broke her arm two months ago. Hoping grandson, Zachary isn't next.

MAY 10, 2019: When my daughter asked what I wanted for Mother's Day, I said, "I have two loving kids with great spouses, three amazing grandkids, a grand-dog and two grand-cats. I have everything."

MAY 11, 2019: I think line dancing was started by a group of women waiting outside a public bathroom.

MAY 12, 2019: My daughter and I spent Mother's Day giggling, cleaning out my kitchen cabinets, and loading her van with the rejects. BEST M. DAY EVER!

MAY 13, 2019: Went to see a heart-warming movie today, called, *Poms*, about women in a retirement center who start a cheerleading squad. Why not!

MAY 14, 2019: I asked my Mary Kay consultants to come to our training meeting without their make-up. We looked like the ghost squad.

MAY 15, 2019: Some days it's hard to remain upbeat in the face of bad things happening in the world around us. If you can't find the sunshine, BE the sunshine.

MAY 16, 2019: It's time to buy a new I-Phone. I can't decide which room of furniture to sell to pay for it.

MAY 17, 2019: Attended the Poetry Society of VA Festival. Looked around the room at the canes, walkers, and gray heads and decided age only matters if you're cheese.

MAY 18, 2019: Woke up this morning thinking it was Friday and a work day. JOY, JOY, when I realized it was Saturday and I could stay in bed.

MAY 19, 2019: The body shop repaired the damage to my car caused by a hit and run driver. Got home and found new scratches caused by the mechanics. *&%#*#

MAY 20, 2019: Went to lunch today and wasn't happy with my menu selection. Should be a calorie refund for things that don't taste as good as we expect.

MAY 21, 2019: I avoid dusting by telling myself, "Dust gives a home that warm, fuzzy feeling."

MAY 22, 2019: There's a shortage of good news in the newspaper. Does that mean there isn't any or good news doesn't sell papers?

MAY 23, 2019: I've been on a cleaning out binge this week. My entertainment center must be where all the video tapes went to die.

MAY 24, 2019: All my gardening friends are happily planting and watering. They tell me a dirty hoe is a happy hoe, but I'm not buying it.

MAY 25, 2019: My talented daughter got a great promotion this week. I'm celebrating the good judgment of her bosses.

MAY 26, 2019: I spent all day trying to make friends with my new I Phone. No matter how many buttons I pushed, it still refused to cozy up with my car.

MAY 27, 2019: I try not to let Memorial Day become a sad day. I like to think my loved ones are having their own cook-out, somewhere out there in the universe.

MAY 28, 2019: I feel helpless when a friend calls and is depressed. I try reminding them, "You are somebody's reason to smile."

MAY 29, 2019: Saw kids cooling off and drinking from a water hose today. Brought back childhood memories of those days before I knew about germs.

MAY 30, 2019: I have a resident lizard who insists on living on my carport. Have learned to make noise before I open door, lest he move into the house.

MAY 31, 2019: I'm tired today. Therefore, I won't!

JUNE

JUNE 1, 2019: Hearts are broken again after another mass shooting, close to home in Virginia Beach. WHY???????????

JUNE 2, 2019: It's Pride Month for my LGBTQ+ friends. I long for a day when they are not persecuted or worse, killed, for just living their lives.

JUNE 3, 2019: Pets and their owners have such a strong connection. One friend told me her dog winks at her. She always winks back, in case it some kind of code.

JUNE 4, 2019: Two deer wandered into my yard at dusk. They ate my Hydrangeas for supper and rose petals for dessert. Not even a thank you.

JUNE 5, 2019: Our Humane Society reminds us, saving one cat will not save the world, but for that one cat, the world will change forever.

JUNE 6, 2019: Did you know ants work as teams? Watched some form a chain and lower a wounded ant from a window sill to the ground, then carry him away.

JUNE 7, 2019: Feels like it's been raining forever. I keep reminding myself-in July and August, when it's 95 and desert-dry, we'll be wishing for those showers.

JUNE 8, 2019: I have a great lawn guy who keeps my two acres mowed and trimmed and warns me where the resident black snake is hanging out.

JUNE 9, 2019: My poetry group is preparing a program for local retirement communities. Will give us a sneak preview of where we're all headed.

JUNE 10, 2019: How did it get to be June already? Seems like I just put away the Christmas decorations.

JUNE 11, 2019: I didn't make it to the gym today. Don't tell anybody, but that makes two years in a row.

JUNE 12, 2019: The USA Women's Soccer team was criticized for "over celebrating" their first win in the 2019 World Cup tournament. WHY NOT CELEBRATE??

JUNE 13, 2019: A carpenter came today to look at my rickety deck steps. He had been working all day and was sprinkled with sawdust / "man glitter."

JUNE 14, 2019: When our grandkids are young, they think we know everything. They don't know we're just really good at making things up.

JUNE 15, 2019: Went to see, *A Funny Thing Happened On the Way to the Forum*. It was great! How do those actors do two shows a day? Standing ovation for them!

JUNE 16, 2019: It's my son's fiftieth birthday. My advice? "Don't ever grow up completely. It's a trap."

JUNE 17, 2019: Life is like a tightrope…confident at the beginning; plugging along in the middle; and trying not to fall off at the end.

JUNE 18, 2019: Had lunch today with a friend who didn't regale me with a long list of aches and pains. Left lunch with a smile instead of indigestion.

JUNE 19, 2019: If you had all the time and money in the world, where would you be? I would be living on an exotic, tropical island with my kids and grandkids around me.

JUNE 20, 2019: My Dad was born on this day in 1913. A wise person once said, "No matter what your relationship with your parents, you miss them when they are gone."

JUNE 21, 2019: Today is the first day of summer. Wind blew my outdoor thermometer face-down on the deck. Felt like joining it after watering plants in the 90-degree heat.

JUNE 22, 2019: Trekked all the way to Kilmarnock for a book show today. More authors than readers but met some nice people and ate some great barbecue.

JUNE 23, 2019: You know you're getting O-L-D when the elevator music is YOUR music.

JUNE 24, 2019: I can't bear the images of hungry kids in cages with no way to clean themselves or brush their teeth. I want to go rescue them. WHO HAVE WE BECOME?

JUNE 25, 2019: It is often said that poetry is the music of language. For me these days, it is the language of frustration, anger, and fear for our future.

JUNE 26, 2019: A friend complained to me that sometimes it takes her all day to get nothing done. I call that Sunday.

JUNE 27, 2019: My daughter loves animals, has a dog and two cats. She says dogs accept you as the boss. Cats treat you like staff.

JUNE 28, 2019: It was nearly 100 degrees today. Summer left its sweaty calling card all over me. May burn my clothes.

JUNE 29, 2019: Another book show today. Again, not many shoppers. Great hot dogs though, and homemade cookies. I may have to give up book shows. Too many calories.

JUNE 30, 2019: I like sharing my daily journey. If you like "riding along" with me, leave a comment on my website or on Face Book. Make my day!

JULY

JULY 1, 2019: One of my neighbors retired recently, happily anticipating a life of leisure. Not so! Now he works for his wife.

JULY 2, 2019: We've been having violent thunderstorms, several nights in a row. My Grandad used to say the thunder was God bowling. God needs to get another hobby!

JULY 3, 2019: We've often been told we need to live in the moment. That's fine if it's pleasant. If not, I'm going to need ice cream.

JULY 4, 2019: My wonderful across-the-street neighbor decorated every yard in ourneighborhood with American flags this morning. May the 4th be with you too!

JULY 5, 2019: My husband used to accuse me of snoring. "Not!" I argued, "I'm dreaming I'm a motorcycle."

JULY 6, 2019: If your wife ever ends an argument with the words, "That's O. K.," BEWARE! She is thinking long and hard about how and when you will pay for your transgressions.

JULY 7, 2019: Single living isn't always conducive to cooking fancy meals. I found the perfect sign today. It says, "I know how to cook. I just don't want to." Amen.

JULY 8, 2019: My windows are rattling again from the latest scary thunderstorm. Really, God, have you thought about taking up painting or poetry?

JULY 9, 2019: Today would have been my mother's 96th birthday. I miss her, especially on shopping days. Nobody loved it more or did it better. "Shop 'till you drop," was her manta.

JULY 10, 2019: Went a little crazy at the Farmers' Market. Carried home enough fruits and veggies to feed a small village. Good news is…most don't have to be cooked. Yah!

JULY 11, 2019: One of my friends recently lost her son very unexpectedly. What can you say? I told her I loved her, and called my own son to tell him the same.

JULY 12, 2019: I was watering the flowers this morning and disturbed a tiny frog hiding in the rocks. It was 90+ degrees, so I watered him too. I think he smiled at me.

JULY 13, 2019: Dear Week-end: I love you!

JULY 14, 2019: I just learned, today is All American Mac and Cheese Day. It's like Flag Day but delicious.

JULY 15, 2019: As I've getting older, I'm gradually getting shorter. Does that mean I'm now fun size?

JULY 16, 2019: Rich people splurging, "I think I'll buy a yacht." Me splurging, "I think I'll add an appetizer."

JULY 17, 2019: I'm on the Board of our Homeowner's Association. I'm still trying to find a resolution that forbids the deer from eating my flowers.

JULY 18, 2019: My poetry group met today. Someone read a "chicken crossing the road" poem… "Chicken. Road. The crossing is within. There is no other side." Profound or bad?

JULY 19, 2019: Sometimes I think we should limit all politicians to two terms-one in office and the second in prison.

JULY 20, 2019: Today is the 50th anniversary of Apollo 11's landing on the moon. I wonder if the astronauts' footprints are still there, along with Old Glory.

JULY 21, 2019: The new theory of decluttering is…hold the item in your hands…if it doesn't give you joy, out it goes! So far, I've thrown out a magnifying mirror and a size eight bathing suit.

JULY 22, 2019: Mother nature sent a mini tornado our way late tonight. Heard the train noise then loud thumps on roof and deck. Too dark to see damage. No leaks so far. Can't sleep.

JULY 23, 2019: Up at daylight. Looks like half a tree on roof. Deck covered in limbs, debris, can't open door onto deck. Called my great lawn guys-on their way. Scared about roof.

JULY 24, 2019: Chris and Terry worked all day yesterday. Got tree off roof and most limbs off deck. Chain saws going all over neighborhood. Roads open. Debris everywhere.

JULY 25, 2019: Roof guys came today. No major damage, Whew! So far, the lawn guys have hauled away four trailer loads and four truckloads of limbs. They estimate two more of each.

JULY 26, 2019: Drove around neighborhood today. Huge trees twisted out of ground and tops of trees twisted off. A couple of houses with trees through roof. So lucky my damage wasn't worse!

JULY 27, 2019: Had a minute to reflect today. Wonder where the deer herd huddled when the trees were blowing away. Saw a doe with three fawns a few days ago. Hope they survived.

JULY 28, 2019: Learned something new about myself today. It only takes one slow-moving person in a three-person-deep grocery aisle to turn me into the Grinch.

JULY 29, 2019: Paid for all the tree removal today. Need to either move to a condo with no trees or get a third job. I'm thinking?! I'm thinking?!

JULY 30, 2019: Another great Tuesday swallowed up by work and responsibilities. Need more ice cream or chocolate, or maybe both.

JULY 31, 2019: Who stole July? Guess I can partially blame it on Mother Nature and her storms. Please Mother, no more temper tantrums for a while. Need peace and quiet.

AUGUST

AUG. 1, 2019: Today is National Girlfriend Day. It's important to keep our girlfriends close. They know too much!

AUG. 2, 2019: Some days I feel like I'm fooling the whole world, walking around cleverly disguised as a responsible adult.

AUG. 3, 2019: Mary Kay Awards Luncheon today. Year #38 as a unit! I love the opportunity to reward and recognize my wonderful team.

AUG. 4, 2019: The Amazon, which provides 20% of the world's oxygen, is burning. Will we only pay attention to the rain forest when WE can't breathe?

AUG. 5, 2019: I miss my three grandchildren who live in Kentucky. Talking to them or sharing pictures and videos is not the same as hugging.

AUG. 6, 2019: Verizon revamped my voice mail system. Why? It works just like the old one, but took me an hour to figure out how to re-set everything.

AUG. 7, 2019: As politicians gear up for the 2020 elections and make wild promises, we, as citizens, must vow to "fight truth decay."

AUG. 8, 2019: Our military continue to be deployed and killed in Afghanistan. What is the end game, and why are we still there?

AUG. 9, 2019: There are conspiracy theorists who believe the world is flat. Don't they know, if it was, cats would have pushed everything off the edge by now.

AUG. 10, 2019: One of my poems will be in the Fall Pen Woman Magazine, joining previous contributors, Eleanor Roosevelt, Pearl S. Buck, Maya Angelou, Hilary Clinton, and many others. Such an honor!

AUG. 11, 2019: One of my dear friends is dying from the complications of ALS. I can't save her, but in her honor, maybe I can brighten someone else's day. These are my goals.

AUG. 12, 2019: Mend a quarrel. Search out a friend I haven't talked to for a while.

AUG. 13, 2019: Keep a promise made but nearly forgotten. Find the time, instead of complaining about being too busy.

AUG. 14, 2019: Dismiss suspicion and replace it with trust. Give the other person the benefit of the doubt. Apologize if wrong.

AUG. 15, 2019: Appreciate. Be kind. Be gentle. Do something to make a child smile.

AUG. 16, 2019: Appreciate the beauty of the earth. Breathe the flower-laden air. Enjoy the sun soaking into weary shoulders.

AUG. 17, 2019: Share treasure with someone less fortunate without expecting thanks.

AUG. 18, 2019: Tell someone you love them.

AUG. 19, 2019: My friend died today of ALS, a disease which robs the victim of voice, mobility, independence, but not soul or heart. She fought till she couldn't fight anymore.

AUG. 20, 2019: On August 20, 1940, my parents eloped. She was 17. He was 27. They hid it from both sets of parents for months. When Mom died, I found some of the love letters they wrote during that time. Lovely to picture your parents as two people in love.

AUG. 21, 2019: A med tech attempted to remove the wax from my ear recently. The ear was damaged. Back to ENT today. Lesson learned…don't do that!

AUG. 22, 2019: Woke up feeling tired. Googled my symptoms. Remedy recommended-Go shopping!

AUG. 23, 2019: Went to see *Lion King* today. Even though I saw the television special about how the film was made, still can't believe those animals are not real.

AUG. 24, 2019: There are war games every night at the military base near my home. Jets fly low. Our windows rattle. But they never tell us who won.

AUG. 25, 2019: Followed an ancient truck on my way home today. Bumper sticker said, "Honk if parts fall off."

AUG. 26, 2019: It's hurricane season and we're beginning to get warnings about possible storms. Hope they stay out to sea and away from all land.

AUG. 27. 2019: I was outside talking to a neighbor, felt something on my foot. Looked down. Was a turtle, crawling over the toe of my shoe. Did he think it was a rock?

AUG. 28, 2019: All my friends are downsizing. I listen to them whining about having to get rid of their stuff. After listening, I have decided to stay in my house and enjoy mine.

AUG. 29, 2019: My cousin is going to a class reunion next week. She planned it after getting an urgent call from a classmate saying, "Must meet soon. Classmates dropping like flies."

AUG. 30, 2019: Can't believe summer is almost over. I just got my summer clothes out last week.

AUG. 31, 2019: I enjoy funny bumper stickers. Saw one today that said, "If you're happy and you know it, it's your meds." Maybe…

SEPTEMBER

SEPT. 1, 2019: Beginning to hear more warnings about Hurricane Dorian. Strikes fear in my heart. Still traumatized from having to rebuild from Hurricane Floyd years ago.

SEPT. 2, 2019: Storm growing. Concerned about Puerto Rico and the Bahamas. Not sure I would be brave enough to live on an island year 'round. Can't swim!

SEPT. 3, 2019: East coast still threatened. Storm moving slow. Expected to be a Category 5. I'm wondering if I'll be able to get out of town for my trip to Arizona on the 10th.

SEPT. 4, 2019: No more procrastinating. Time to start putting away all the loose stuff on the deck, porch. I know the drill. We will at least get heavy rain and high winds.

SEPT. 5, 2019: The Bahamas were pummeled with winds up to 185 miles an hour. News pictures are heart-breaking. Impact here expected tomorrow but tropical storm strength.

SEPT. 6, 2019: Dreaded Dorian was a non-event for us, some light wind, a little rain. Grateful! Hundreds of people missing in the Bahamas. Death count expected to rise.

SEPT. 7, 2019: Friends up and down the East Coast reporting in-lots of trees down and power outages but everyone safe. Lots of clean-up ahead. Bright, sunny day!

SEPT. 8, 2019: Read a wonderful thing today. A bar in Florida that was decorated with $1 bills, stapled to walls, took them down and sent $13,961 to Hurricane Dorian relief.

SEPT 9, 2019: Can finish packing for Arizona trip. Charlotte airport up and running. No problems getting out of Richmond. Whew!!

SEPT. 10, 2019: WESTWARD HO!! Richmond to Charlotte to Phoenix with my buddy, Kaye. 88 degrees in Phoenix (115 yesterday!) Friend, Vivien, waiting. Let the vacation begin!

SEPT. 11, 2019: My friend, Viv, lives in the quaint, little town of Cottonwood, AZ. She had to work today so we wandered through the Main Street shops and admired the cowboys, complete with tight jeans, scuffed boots, and Stetsons. Nothing wrong with looking.

SEPT. 12, 2019: Off today for a 5-day trip, beginning in the red rock magic of Sedona, traveling north to the mountains of Flagstaff, and ending the day in the Petrified Forest and the Painted Desert. Blues and burgundy of the desert at sunset, illuminated by a full moon. WOW!

SEPT. 13, 2019: "Shop till we dropped" morning in Gallup, New Mexico. So much gorgeous Indian jewelry-so little time! On to Sky City, Acoma Pueblo, perched high on a plateau overlooking the desert. More about that in my new travel book, out soon.

SEPT. 14, 2019: Hubbell Trading Post and Cameron Trading post in one morning-more jewelry we couldn't resist. On to Canyon De Chelly and Monument Valley in Canyonlands. Watched the sunset shower golden pink over the buttes. Breathtaking!

SEPT. 15, 2019: Grand Canyon Day!!! A new, amazing view around every turn of the South Rim drive. Late lunch at the famed El Tovar Hotel perched on the edge of the canyon. Sunset bathes the canyon in shades of blue, pink and silver and then DARK. Temps drop to 45.

SEPT. 16, 2019: The little gold mining town of Jerome, its houses sliding down the hill, an inch a year, is one of my favorite places. It is an artists' mecca. Lunch in the Grand Hotel on top of the mountain. It's called The Asylum. I'm told ghosts walk at night. Didn't stay to see.

SEPT. 17, 2019: Weary but happy travelers piled ourselves and our dirty clothes into Viv's house in Cottonwood. Kaye and I collapsed for nearly a whole day. Poor Viv had to go to work. We kept calling to be sure she was awake. Social workers can't sleep on the job.

SEPT. 18, 2019: Kaye and I on the road again with my friends Jim and Jeannie, who live in the cowboy town of Prescott. We toured the bars of Whiskey Row, which now house gift shops and restaurants, and took pics of the town square. Could be right out of *Oklahoma*.

SEPT. 19, 2019: Jim drove us back over the mountain to Cottonwood while Jeannie and I reminisced about our days together in Williamsburg. She started our Sweet Adeline Chapter. She still sings. I don't, and miss it. Took Viv to dinner to make up for having to work all day.

SEPT. 20, 2019: PARTY DAY! Viv has invited some of her artist and writer friends for an "Artistic Pot Luck." So many talented, interesting people. Viv is an amazing artist herself. She has created most of the covers for my books and illustrated a couple of the children's books. I read some poetry. Kaye talked about her beautiful cards. Great way to end our adventure.

SEPT. 21, 2019: One more day! Driving to Phoenix to meet some high school friends of mine, Sandra and Richard. Sandra and I grew up together in W. VA, three houses apart and were always best friends. Good to hug and reminisce. One last gabfest with Viv in the hotel. Fly tomorrow.

SEPT. 22, 2019: Teary goodbyes at airport. Phoenix to Charlotte to Richmond. Perfect flight. Shannon there to meet us and drive our tired bodies home to Williamsburg. She even stocked the frig. Daughters are the best!! Dreams of red rocks, pink sunsets, and canyons, so grand!

SEPT. 23, 2019: Reality! Phone calls to return, dirty laundry, piles of mail to sift through. Also, a 3-hour time difference to get used to, again! But memories-great, fun memories, to fill tonight's dreams.

SEPT. 24, 2019: Mary Kay meeting. Glad to see all my friends. We have a beach trip coming up in October, so lots of planning to do. And new holiday products-Christmas, already? Oh my!

SEPT. 25, 2019: Fun to meet with my Creative Writing group today. Assignment was to write about something we enjoyed from the summer. I shared some of the highlights from trip.

SEPT. 26, 2019: Just noticed yesterday was National Voter Registration Day. You are registered, right? People fought and died to win that privilege for us. YOU MUST VOTE!

SEPT. 27, 2019: Chris, the nice man who takes care of my lawn, nearly lost his adult son while I was gone. He was hospitalized with a collapsed lung from vaping. Hard lesson!

SEPT. 28, 2019: Everyone is talking about the presidential impeachment investigation. Bottom line-no one is above the law, not even the president.

SEPT. 29, 2019: Went to see Downton Abbey today. Loved every minute of it. I could get used to living in a castle. I would especially love having a cook to do all the meals. When?

SEPT. 30, 2019: My new travel book, *Road Trip*, is in the final stages of production. Stay tuned for a debut date. I'm super excited about it!!!

OCTOBER

OCT. 1, 2019: I want to wake up tomorrow to ZERO bad news, just adorable cat videos.

OCT. 2, 2019: My yard is covered in leaves-not pretty, yellow and orange leaves, but dead brown ones. Haven't had rain for weeks. May be time for the naked rain dance.

OCT. 3, 2019: There was a massacre in my back yard today. A red fox got two of my neighbor's pet chickens-white feathers everywhere. I know, nature, and all that, but still sad.

OCT. 4, 2019: Have been working on edits of my new travel book, *Road Trip*. Can't wait to get it finished and off to the printer. Will be out in November.

OCT. 5, 2019: Packing today for a trip to Corolla in Outer Banks, N. C., with three of my girlfriends. Weather fool is predicting rain all week. Rain here, please, not there.

OCT. 6, 2019: Casa Del Sol is our home for the week-a gorgeous 5 BR mansion on the Sound, complete with swimming pool, exquisite furnishings, and glorious sunsets. Happy dance!

OCT. 7, 2019: Visited the Corolla Lighthouse. Checked out the beach for wild horses. Saw none. Rain predicted tomorrow. Gorgeous sunset over the Sound.

OCT. 8, 2019: Neither rain nor gusty wind kept the Four Beach Babes from exploring the south end of Outer Banks today, pigging out on delicious seafood, and SHOPPING.

OCT. 9, 2019: Still raining and windy, but decided to drive to Manteo on Roanoke Island anyway. Visited the Elizabethan Gardens and then drove down to Bodie Island. Had homemade ice cream on the way home. Yum!

OCT. 10, 2019: Did an interesting tour of the Whalehead Club in Historic Corolla. It was built in 1923 as a 21,000 sq. ft. hunting lodge, complete with indoor plumbing and a saltwater pool in basement. We all enjoyed the art deco furnishings.

OCT. 11, 2019: Vacation almost over-too soon. Great week of seeing Outer Banks, rainy beach walks, shopping, delicious food, hibernating with our books, and amazing conversations.

OCT. 12, 2019: My girlfriends went home yesterday and my top Mary Kay consultants arrived last night. What to do today-beach walk, shop, lunch-how about all of the above, plus dinner out? Yes! Gorgeous sunshiny day. Game Nite tonight!

OCT. 13, 2019: Goodbye to Casa Del Sol and homeward bound. Rain started as we got to Williamsburg. We cheered. Need it so badly. My yard looks like the Arizona desert.

OCT. 14, 2019: Still raining. and I'm still dancing! Some people celebrate Columbus, the Pirate, today. I celebrate Indigenous Peoples' Day in honor of all the native people he was responsible for killing, and the societies he and his explorers destroyed.

OCT. 15, 2019: I approved the cover for my new book, *Road Trip*, today. It's colorful and fun. My publisher, Jeanne Johansen, did an amazing job on it. Can't wait for all of you to see it.

OCT. 16, 2019: Day 3 of home from vacation, and haven't even had time to unpack. My critique group read stories today about the things they are grateful for. We are all very blessed.

OCT. 17, 2019: My poetry group, the James City Poets met today. We've become a traveling show, doing programs for the retirement facilities in town. We are a hit! Who knew seniors would love our poetry so much? It's been a heart-warming experience.

OCT. 18, 2019: My patio doors off the deck need to be replaced. I've ordered the doors and am waiting for an installation date. My biggest fear is wildlife like mice and lizards sneaking in while the guys are working. Had a snake in the house last winter. Don't want to repeat that!

OCT. 19, 2019: I love potluck dinners! It's such fun to sample everyone's specialties. Our neighborhood dinner was tonight and it did not disappoint. We have great cooks in Elmwood.

OCT. 20, 2019: I had a lot of stuff to do today. Scrapbooked my Arizona trip instead. Now I have a lot of stuff to do tomorrow. Oh well...

OCT. 21, 2019: The early bird can have the worm because worms are gross and mornings should start after nine.

OCT. 22, 2019: I know it's Tuesday but I like Fridays better so can I just declare it Friday and move directly to the week-end?

OCT. 23, 2019: Dentist appointment this morning. My teeth are so clean, I don't think I should ever eat again.

OCT. 24, 2019: Today would have been my husband, Don's, 90th birthday. He's been gone for six years and I still miss that crazy, wonderful man!

OCT. 25, 2019: Still waiting for my new sliding glass doors to be installed. Will make one more polite call today, then…

OCT. 26, 2019: Friday finally got here, so I'm thinking of celebrating by honoring Don's favorite motto, "Eat your dessert first!" I'm thinking…cheesecake.

OCT. 27, 2019: I keep hearing the phrase, "History is repeating itself," all day long on the news. If it does repeat itself, I'm getting a dinosaur.

OCT. 28, 2019: Had lunch with a friend today at the local Indian restaurant. We especially like their rice pudding so decided food with friends has zero calories. Good call?

OCT. 29, 2019: DID YOU KNOW…the internet is 50 years old today?? Sometimes I feel 100 when I'm trying to figure how to navigate it.

OCT. 30, 2019: Today is my daughter, Shannon's, birthday. Who knew that tiny little darling with the mop of black hair would grow up to be amazing-beautiful, smart, talented, and most of all, loving and caring. Lucky me!

OCT. 31, 2019: It's Halloween!! I love seeing the little, neighborhood kids in their super hero and princess costumes. Brings a smile every time the doorbell rings.

NOVEMBER

NOV. 1, 2019: If it's November, all you turkeys need to run for your lives! The cooks are coming for you with stuffing and gravy.

NOV. 2, 2019: On the first Saturday of every month, we invite poets to come to the library to inspire us with their creativity. Today, Virginia's Poet Laureate, Henry Hart, read for us. Great!!

NOV. 3, 2019: Patience is what you demonstrate when there are too many witnesses.

NOV. 4, 2019: Do you ever feel that you spend much too much time in doctor's offices? Me too! Today, it was eye examination time. At least we can leave our clothes on for that one.

NOV. 5, 2019: Today is Election Day. I don't understand people who take that right for granted and stay home. We owe it to those who fought to win that right, to show up.

NOV. 6, 2019: The Chesapeake Bay Writers held their Annual Awards Luncheon today. One of my poems won First Place, and a non-fiction article won a Second Place award. Shock and awe!

NOV. 7, 2019: Work? Really? Didn't I just do that yesterday?

NOV. 8, 2019: Had lunch with a friend today. Had to yell to hear each other. Is it just me or is the music in restaurants outrageously LOUD? Won't go there again.

NOV. 9, 2019: I did my first book signing at the downtown Barnes & Noble today. Was fun to see my name on the front door as I entered. Nice people, nice day, even sold a few books.

NOV. 10, 2019: I lead a little group called Wonder Women. We gather at my house every couple of months to have fun, share good food and our stories, and support each other.

NOV. 11, 2019: Had a fun, creative day today, setting up Mary Kay displays for my holiday open house. Now, if I can just get the customers to come and shop…

NOV. 12, 2019: It SNOWED today. Surprise! Huge flakes all afternoon, covering the ground. Roads melted off but everything else is decorated white for Christmas. Isn't it just November??

NOV. 13, 2019: Yard still a fairyland, and too cold to melt much today. But roads clear so can get out to run errands and make deliveries. Too bad! A day by the fireplace would be nice.

NOV. 14, 2019: Saw a good movie today, *Last Christmas*, I am a movie buff, would go more often if it wasn't for the parking and long walk to theatre, etc. Movies on TV, just not the same.

NOV. 15, 2019: Today is my granddaughter, Adaline's, birthday. Can't believe she is twelve already. She now has her own phone so we can text back and forth. Fun for me!

NOV. 16, 2019: The Williamsburg Players did a version of *Cheaper By the Dozen* today. Somehow, they found twelve adorable, talented kids who brought down the house. Impressive.

NOV. 17, 2019: My sliding glass doors finally got installed. Hopefully, no lizards, snakes, or squirrels entered the premises during the process.

NOV. 18, 2019: The impeachment hearings continue this week. I'm so impressed with the hard work and research done by the committee. I repeat, not even a president is above the law.

NOV. 19, 2019: Full day of Mary Kay shoppers today. It's fun to visit with my customers/friends and catch up on all the news. Everyone went home with full bags of goodies.

NOV. 20, 2019: Are you old enough to have dialed a rotary phone while listening to an 8-track? I am!

NOV. 21, 2019: Scientists say the universe is made up of protons, neutrons, and electrons. They forgot to mention morons, like the one who cut me off in traffic today.

NOV. 22, 2019: Every time I hear about a foreign country threatening us-North Korea, Iran, etc., I wonder why we don't stop sending them aid, and let them hate us for free.

NOV. 23, 2019: There is a restaurant in town, Victoria's, that fills its rooms with nutcrackers to celebrate the holidays-tiny ones, life-size ones-dozens of them. It's my happy place in Dec.

NOV. 24, 2019: If you plan on cooking a large turkey on Thursday, today is the day to move it from freezer to frig. The experts say it takes five days to thaw. Really?

NOV. 25, 2019: OK, I called my friend who's cooking Thanksgiving dinner for Shannon and me, and gave her the five-day turkey thawing prognosis. Guess what she said, "Really????"

NOV. 26, 2019: When my sister-in-law was a newly-wed, she wanted to impress our family by cooking Thanksgiving dinner. She stuffed the turkey with bread crumbs which stayed dry and hard. We crunched and told her how great it was. The next year, it really was great.

NOV. 27, 2019: All of my Mary Kay shoppers cancelled today. Guess they're still working on that turkey.

NOV. 28, 2019: Turkey Day finally arrived! Shared great conversation and a delicious dinner with our friend, Kaye. She said experts were right. Took turkey five days to thaw.

NOV. 29, 2019: Today is daughter, Shannon, and spouse, A. J.'s anniversary. I'm so happy those two found each other. This time, Cupid got it right.

NOV. 30, 2019: I end the month full of gratitude for loving family, supportive friends, and a brain that can still fill the page with happy nonsense. Life is good! My t-shirt says so.

DECEMBER

DEC. 1, 2019: I just heard Walmart is marketing Kentucky Fried Chicken-scented logs for the fireplace. Better keep an eye on your dog!

DEC. 2, 2019: Thought you might enjoy a poetry lesson for December, to get your mind off all the shopping, baking, wrapping, card writing, screaming, etc. Read on…

DEC. 3, 2019: A Haiku is a three-line poem. Line 1 has 5 syllables, line 2 has 7, and line 3 has 5. Ready? Here we go, count syllables with me…

DEC. 4, 2019: Dashing through the mall…with a list that's two miles long…Christmas Eve nightmare.

DEC. 5, 2019: Here's another. Christmas colors shine…We love their diversity…Why not in people?

DEC. 6, 2019: You'll like this one. Keep counting. You better be good…Elf on the shelf is watching…Let's blindfold that guy!

DEC. 7, 2029: Christmas is giving…of love, of gifts, of ourselves…Make it last all year.

DEC. 8, 2019: Window panes glisten…Carols fill the silent night…Wish peace would linger.

DEC. 9, 2019: Christmas is fruitcake…Christmas is time with family…Some are fruitcakes too.

DEC. 10, 2019: See how easy it is to write Haikus? Your turn! Write one and put it in the comment section of my website, sharoncanfielddorsey.com. Can't wait to discover new poetic talent. That means you!

DEC. 11, 2019: The clock is ticking. The traffic is terrible. I burned the cookies. There aren't enough hours in the day. Sound familiar? What happened to peace on earth????

DEC. 12, 2019: Again, I retreat to poetry. This lesson is even easier than the Haikus I taught you earlier. These are six-word poems. Yes, just six. Read and relax…

DEC. 13, 2019: Carols fill the air. Sing along.

DEC. 14, 2019: Dashing through the snow. OOPS! Down.

DEC. 15, 2019: Presents bought earlier. Where are they?

DEC. 16, 2019: Santa, I've been good. Pinky swear!

DEC. 17, 2019: Christmas letters. Paper hugs from friends.

DEC. 18, 2019: Found last year's fruitcake. Re-gift quickly.

DEC. 19, 2019: Christmas through grandchildren's eyes. The best.

DEC. 20, 2019: Don't ignore homeless. Could be you.

DEC. 21, 2019: Love is best gift. Spread around.

DEC. 22, 2019: Just learned that grandson, Zachary, has the flu. So sad for him. Don't know what that will do to son, Steven's plan to arrive here on Sunday, the 29th. All up in air.

DEC. 23, 2019: Zachary still sick and quarantined to room. Steven put up twinkle lights and brought in small tree for him, even arranged a face-time call from Santa. Technology rocks!

DEC. 24, 2019: Steven sent fun video of kids opening Secret Santa gifts. Zachary's fever gone. Whew! I'm wrapping gifts and watching holiday movies. Happiness is anticipation!

DEC. 25, 2019: HO, HO, HO!! Shannon and I had a lovely day together-cooked, ate too much, opened presents, and face-timed with Steven and family all day. As I said- technology rocks!!

DEC. 26, 2019: Good news! Zachary much better, so plans still on for our Sunday Christmas. My artist friend, Vivien, from AZ, will be here tomorrow for a friend gathering. Can't wait. So fun!

DEC. 27, 2019: What a fun day! Friends came and went all afternoon with gifts and snacks. Vivien hasn't been home for two years, so it was great to be together again. Endless chatter!

DEC. 28, 2019: Cooking and last-minute present wrapping today. Steven, Amy, and grandkids will be here tomorrow. Shannon and A. J. both off from work so we can all be together.

DEC. 29, 2019: Happiness is having all my family home and around the Christmas tree. Chaos reigns as we all open presents, ooh and ahh, then share Christmas dinner. Smiling!!

DEC 30, 2019: Listen…running feet, giggles, Legos snapping into place (their favorite presents!), then hide and seek in the yard, followed by homemade cookies. Happy dance!!

DEC. 31, 2019: Clock strikes 10 a.m. The Santa SUV, loaded with kids and presents, is headed to grandparent visit #2 in Roanoke. Still smiling as I tackle the Xmas clutter left behind.

JANUARY, 2020

JAN. 1, 2020: Happy New Year! We made it to 2020! Now if we can just remember to write it on our checks… Time for resolutions. I resolve to write one a day for ten days. Join me with your own?????

JAN. 2, 2020: I will do less things I dislike and more things that make me happy, like going to the movies instead of dusting. I dusted. It came back. Not falling for that again!

JAN. 3, 2020: I will spend more time with friends who laugh, and less with those who constantly complain.

JAN. 4, 2020: I will read the six books stacked up on my nightstand instead of watching the bad, awful, rotten, stinkin' news all the time.

JAN. 5, 2020: I will not say bad words about the deer, rabbits and groundhogs who lunch on my shrubs and flowers. MAYBE.

JAN. 6, 2020: I will write more poetry and listen to more jazz.

JAN. 7, 2020: I will re-watch all the Avengers movies on Disney+ without guilt. After all, Shannon gave me the channel for Christmas. I OWE it to her to watch every single one!

JAN. 8, 2020: I will pay at least one compliment a day to someone who needs one. Think of the smiles I'll collect!

JAN. 9, 2020: I'll do more things to help the planet- including harassing friends who do not recycle. It's a small thing. We can all do it and it makes a BIG difference.

JAN. 10, 2020: I will encourage everyone I know to vote and I will actively support candidates I believe in. Democracy is worth saving. Our ancestors expect that of us.

JAN. 11, 2020: I will assume every day could be my last, and savor the moments, large and small.

JAN. 12, 2020: I'm making good on one of my resolutions, the one about compliments. Thank you for faithfully reading my blog. YOU have great taste!

JAN. 13, 2020: Another one-six deer jumped across the road in front of me as I was coming home yesterday. I still cursed, but silently. Can I count that?

JAN. 14, 2020: Went to the movies to see *Little Women* on $5 day. Ticket line out to the street and no place to park. A friend found a spot and stood in it 'til I got there. THAT'S a friend!

JAN. 15, 2020: Steven, Shannon and I have always been big Star Wars fans. Steven took all three kids to see *Rise of Skywalker*, carrying on the family tradition. Zachary loved it, girls, not so much. I gave Steven points for trying. *Frozen 2*, next time, I guess.

JAN. 16, 2020: The Christmas decorations are finally down. Yah me! Sometimes they're around 'til Valentine's Day. When they start getting dusty-it's time. I do miss them though.

JAN. 17, 2020: The impeachment trial starts in the Senate next Tuesday. Would like to be there to watch those old guys falling asleep because they're not allowed to talk or use their phones.

JAN. 18, 2020: We've had such a warm winter, the ornamental trees are starting to bloom. Hope they don't get their pretty pink blossoms frozen.

JAN. 19, 2020: Speaking of plants, saw a cup the other day with a picture of a dandelion that said, "Some see weeds, I see wishes." Are you a cup-half-full person or a cup-half-empty one?

JAN. 20, 2020: Note the date. Has to be a lucky day. Should go out and buy some winning lottery tickets or get married. One is as likely to happen as the other. In other words, NOT.

JAN. 21, 2020: I have a birthday coming up next month. I confess, I thought getting old would take longer.

JAN. 22, 2020: I just learned my brother, Carl, has a tumor on his tonsils, probably cancerous. Wrote a blog about his courageous battles with health issues. This one is really scary.

JAN. 23, 2020: Had lunch today with my friend of 40 years, Carlton. Our birthdays are a month apart and he still teases me every year about being younger. Forever friends are the best!

JAN. 24, 2020: Hair-cut day! It seems my hair always looks its best on the day I'm about to cut it. Can be terrible the day before but on hair-cut day, it says, "Why are you doing this to me?"

JAN 25, 2020: What's the best thing about Saturday??? It's not a Monday through Friday work day! Second best thing-I can hang out in my sweats all day.

JAN. 26, 2020: My movie theatre rents space to a local church on Sundays. It's perfect! You can go to an R-Rated film and be forgiven on the way out.

JAN. 27, 2020: This is the strangest January. Temperatures of 70 – 80. People wandering around in shorts. Maybe Williamsburg is the new Florida.

JAN 28, 2020: Being over seventy doesn't mean you can't learn something new every day. It just means you may forget three others.

JAN. 29, 2020: Some people are like clouds. When they disappear, it's a beautiful day.

JAN. 30, 2020: Went to the movies to see *Dr. Doolittle* today. It was sweet and funny family entertainment, so didn't need to be forgiven on the way out.

JAN. 31, 2020: My brother is still waiting to get the results of his biopsy. Why does it take so long? The uncertainty is so hard on the patient and family alike.

FEBRUARY

FEB. 1. 2020: Have been watching the impeachment trial of Donald Trump. It's sad how divided our country is. I keep remembering Barack Obama saying, "We are not red states and blue states -we are the United States." What happened to those shining moments of hope?

FEB. 2, 2020: One of my friends flew off to New Zealand today for two weeks. A little envious. It's on my travel wish list. Flight takes over sixteen hours. That's a lot of in-flight movies!

FEB. 3, 2020: A surprise! One of my essays won Third place in the National League of American Pen Women Annual Contest. There were over 300 entries. I'm so honored! Title is, *Well-behaved Women Seldom Make History*.

FEB. 4, 2020: My brother, Carl, finally got the results of his tests. It is cancer. Doctor recommends surgery, but must have it approved by the Surgical Board. Waiting again.

FEB. 5, 2020: Saw this on a sign today, "ME…I'm finally happy with my life. LIFE…LOL. Just wait a sec." So true, so true!

FEB. 6, 2020: The president was acquitted yesterday. Only one republican found him guilty. Many others agreed and said that he was guilty, but refused to stand against him.

FEB. 7, 2020: Watched some of the caucus gatherings in Iowa tonight. Lots of college-age people. One young volunteer offered to do her friend's homework if she'd caucus for her candidate. Friend agreed. Strange way to nominate a president!

FEB. 8, 2020: No winners announced yet in Iowa. Problems with the new app they tried to use. Oh, the glories of technology!

FEB. 9, 2020: I'm going to stop asking, "How dumb can you get?" People seem to be taking it as a challenge.

FEB. 10, 2020: After watching several debates, I think I should receive an award for keeping my mouth shut when there's so much more that needs to be said.

FEB. 11, 2020: The coronavirus is spreading. Guess it's time to give up handshakes, hugs, and breathing in the same space as other people.

FEB. 12, 2020: Common sense seems to be so rare these days, it's kind of like a superpower.

FEB. 13, 2020: A friend and I went out to lunch today to celebrate our February birthdays together. The staff saw the gifts, and came over to sing to us, AND give us a free piece of pie. Yah, Chickahominy House!

FEB. 14, 2020: Ran in the drug store to get a prescription this evening. Line at check-out was full of anxious men with cards and candy. At least they remembered, last minute.

FEB. 15, 2020: My brother, Carl, finally got a date for his cancer surgery, March 9. It's a long time to wait when you're in so much pain, but was the earliest the surgeon could do it.

FEB. 16, 2020: My cousin, Ginger, offered to drive me to WV today, to visit with Carl on his birthday tomorrow. Very appreciative. My back issues make it hard to do the five-hour drive. Weather good and we are on our way!

FEB. 17, 2020: Good visit yesterday, and my favorite down-home food for dinner-pinto beans and cornbread. Carl insisted on cooking, buzzing around in his Jazzy chair.

FEB. 18, 2020: Birthday dinner last night at a great Chinese restaurant with Carl and cousins. Was not easy for him or for wife, Debi, who is recuperating from hip surgery, but we had fun.

FEB. 19, 2020: Home again. Tired, but so glad I was able to go up for a visit. It's hard to see someone you love in pain and at risk. I treasure the time we had together, even though my baby brother beat me at Scrabble. Badly!!

FEB. 20, 2020: Thank you for going on this year-long, day-at-a-time, journey with me that began on my birthday, last February 20. It was a monumental year in so many ways. Now, unexpectedly, we face unknown health challenges from the Covid Virus. Let's hope our scientists are smart and our leaders are wise.

2025 FOOTNOTE:

Over a million people died in the United States during the two-year Covid Pandemic.

WHEN THE WORLD SHUT DOWN

PART 9

BEEN THERE - DONE THAT
HAPPY DANCE!

History Repeats Itself

And people stayed at home
And read books
And listened
And they rested
And did exercises
And made art and played
And learned new ways of being
And stopped and listened more deeply
Someone meditated, someone prayed
Someone met their shadow
And people began to think differently
And people healed
And in the absence of people who
Lived in ignorant ways that were
Dangerous, meaningless and heartless,
The earth also began to heal
And when the danger ended and
People found themselves
They grieved for the dead
And made new choices
And dreamed of new visions
And created new ways of living
And began to heal the earth
Just as they were healed.

All of this sounds very familiar because this was our life for two years, but this anonymous poem was actually written in 1869 during the fourth cholera epidemic of the 19th century. That epidemic lasted from 1863-1875. The first cholera pandemic emerged in India in 1817.

The same poem was reprinted during the 1919 influenza virus (Spanish Flu) pandemic that resulted in 50 million deaths worldwide and approximately 675,000 in the U. S.

It appears history does repeat itself about every 100 years:

1720 Bubonic Plague

1820 Cholera

1920 Spanish Flu

2020 Coronavirus

Let's hope, this time around, we do create new visions, heal the earth, and heal each other.

A Very Scary Fairy Tale

Once upon a time, there was a beautiful land,
suddenly attacked by a silent, invisible enemy.
Thousands of citizens perished.

The People could no longer go to work or school.
They were quarantined at home with their families,
pets, assorted electronic devices and Netflix.
What *were* they to do?

First, they cooked all the food in their freezers,
including, in some cases, items hoarded since Y2K.
When they ran out of freezer dinners, they foraged in the
pantry to create culinary surprises from lima beans and Jello.

They cleaned their overflowing closets and drawers,
unearthing treasures, taxes from 1980 - 2019, and junk.
The trash and re-cycle workers left them hate mail,
but they kept right on pillaging and purging.

About week six, they emerged to discover SPRING with
bright, clear skies and no scent of exhaust fumes.
Bird song filled the air, daffodils danced on strong legs,
and the deer in the back yard had stopped coughing.

The people of the land were so delighted, they
volunteered to stay indoors a few more weeks,
in exchange for toilet paper.

Grocery Shopping In The Age Of Covid-19

Mostly, I don't-shop, that is. My personal shopper daughter, Shannon, hunts and gathers groceries on Saturday and drops her findings off on my carport. I try to make my list as simple as possible-no specific brands, etc. Every Saturday is a new adventure, depending on what the store is out of and what substitutions she decides to make. I've learned to love the surprises and the new cooking challenges. There is always a guilty pleasure, like ice cream that wasn't on the list or fresh flowers. I'm getting very spoiled!

Yesterday, I decided to venture out to the local Food Lion on my own. I chose my shopping time with safety uppermost in mind, so arrived at 8:30 a.m., during the special time allotted for "chronologically disadvantaged" people like me. My fellow shoppers were all carefully masked and gloved and concentrating fully on the task at hand. I was hoping for a *find*, so went first to the aisles that my daughter tells me are normally empty.

Disappointment-no paper towels or toilet paper or Clorox. Also, no cans of Campbells chicken broth which we both like for a favorite rice/mushroom casserole. BUT, in the rice aisle, two bags of jasmine rice which has been out of stock for weeks. I snatch one for me and one for Shannon and hurry to pasta. "Slim pickin's," as my Mom would have said, but I add two boxes to my cart and move on to canned vegetables. Lots of vacant space on the shelves, especially in the beans section. Is the whole town living on beans and rice? Maybe it's just as well we're not all hanging out together! The fruit shelves are similarly sparse.

One of my goals was to find some Extra Strength Tylenol, which has been harder to track down than Big Foot. Bingo! Two boxes on the shelf, but each securely locked into a special container that can only be opened by the cashier and sporting a sign, "One Per Customer." O. K., I can live with that. Who knew pain relief medication would someday be locked up like diamond and gold jewelry? I wander up and down the aisles and gather what I can, then fill in the gaps with fresh veggies and fruits, which seem abundant. Proud of my bounty, I stand on the big black X, separating customers, until it's my turn at the check-out. The cashier behind the plexiglass barrier, in her mask and gloves, thanks me for shopping at Food Lion. I thank her for working at Food Lion, so I **can** shop. Her eyes smile at me. I'm out of there. Bah humbug!

March, 2020

Six Feet Apart

My *personal shopper* daughter
leaves two bags of groceries by my
side door, then texts me, "I'm here."

We chat for a minute across the slab
of concrete. She says, "I wish I could
hug you." I reply, "I'm just glad to see
your beautiful face." She waves and leaves.

I spray the paper bags with Lysol, carry
them inside, and put the cans and boxes
in the pantry on a dedicated shelf.
I won't use them for several days.

I scrub my hands with soap, while singing
"Happy Birthday" twice. I use my small
stash of Clorox wipes to clean the doorknobs.

This is my new coronavirus normal as a
chronologically-disadvantaged human.

March, 2020

Scenes from the Battlefield…

Seeing flags around the country at half-staff for coronavirus victims.

Cringing at news of two women fighting over toilet paper in Walmart.

Watching in fear as my son-in-law goes to work every day.

Being selfishly grateful that my daughter can work from home.

Reassuring my fifty-year-old son that he WILL find a job after lay-off.

Thanking grocery store clerks behind plexiglass, wearing masks and gloves.

Empathizing with the staggering numbers of unemployed applying for benefits.

Absorbing the rare sight of restaurants, theatres, shopping malls-dark.

Noticing parks and playgrounds roped off and monitored by police.

Waving to my daughter as she leaves groceries and blows me a kiss.

Watching my nine-year-old granddaughter's virtual birthday party.

Worrying about friends in assisted living centers being cared for by workers with no masks and no gloves.

Connecting with friends all over the country who are in lock-down, like me.

Thinking about my friend in the hospital on a ventilator, battered by the virus.

Feeling my heart sink when my brother, hospitalized for cancer surgery, is exposed to the virus by his nurse.

Watching scenes of refrigerated trucks filled with bodies of people who died without the comfort of loved ones around them.

Being grateful for people sewing masks, shopping for seniors, caring by distancing.

Appreciating the safety of my home and the love of my friends and family.

Wondering when and how it will end and who we will be when it does.

June, 2020

Remember When...

People hugged and shook hands without feeling guilty.
Lunching out was a treat, not a possible death sentence.
School and teachers were taken for granted.
Clerks in grocery stores were barely noticed.
Walking into a store did not trigger anxiety.
Toilet paper was just another grocery list item.
Extra Strength Tylenol was not kept in locked boxes.
A movie date did not require Clorox spray and wipes.
We were always promising to clean our cluttered closets.
We could stop to gas up without masking and gloving up.
Meetings were in person, not on Zoom or Facetime.
We could hug our kids and grandkids without fear.
Seniors were not locked up in retirement centers.
The nice man repairing the stove did not strike fear.
Masks were for Halloween, not political statements.
Birthday cards got delivered in less than two weeks.
Miles-long lines for free food were non-existent.
A $1,400 government check wasn't a necessity against homelessness.
500,000+ Americans were still alive, loving and being loved.
We didn't know our lives were about to change forever.
Remember January, 2020?

March, 2021

FOOD IS LOVE

Some of my earliest memories are of my mother building a fire in our big, iron cooking stove so she could sizzle bacon and eggs and bake fluffy, crisp-on the-bottom biscuits for our early morning breakfasts before school. I also recall my grandma dressing me in an apron that dragged to my ankles, then perching me on a stool so I could carefully cut boiled eggs in half to make deviled eggs. I was six. I didn't, at that age, equate any of those things to love, but it was.

My first date at *Sweet Sixteen* was a school dance followed by hot dogs and pineapple milkshakes at the local drive-in. My future husband and I repeated that meal every Saturday night during our high school romance. Those two foods still conjure up memories of first love, although the actuality now would probably result in acute indigestion.

Looking through old scrapbooks recently, I was reminded of a favorite pizza place where my kids and I gathered with their friends for birthday parties or sometimes, just a day out to celebrate good grades or commiserate over disappointments. Pizza was love. Still is. My daughter and I couldn't spend Mother's Day together this year because of pandemic distancing. So, she brought me a pizza from my favorite restaurant, eyes misty over her mask as she handed it to me. It was the perfect gift.

Our lives are filled with examples of love, celebrated with food-wedding cakes, ice cream birthday cakes, luncheons with friends, popcorn with family on movie nights, neighbors bringing casseroles when a loved one is sick or dies. At Eastertime this year, a neighbor and her children made egg-shaped cookies, decorated them, and hung bags of them on our doors. Love!

As I watch the dreaded newscast every night, I am touched by the many food-related love stories…

> Volunteers working long hours to fill food boxes and bags for the jobless.

Farmers donating produce which they no longer can sell, to fill those boxes and bags.

Restaurants and school kitchens cooking meals for the hungry.

Ordinary, extraordinary people paying for groceries for the person behind them in line, and walking away, expecting nothing.

School bus drivers delivering lunches to children on their route.

An out-of-town friend ordering a special meal to be delivered to his buddy in an assisted living facility, who hasn't been allowed to leave his room for weeks.

The aroma of fresh bread wafting across the land as we return to our baking roots, as evidenced by current flour shortages in grocery stores.

I'm a believer-food is love.

June, 2020

TIME-LIKE A PICNIC

Confession-I loved the early pandemic isolation.
There! I said it! I liked time that was mine alone,
like a picnic laid out before me, just waiting to be
savored, any time, any way I chose to partake of it.

At first, I felt strange, not living strictly by the clock,
cancelling lunches with friends, even appointments
with doctors. My guilt-erasing justification-we
had to follow the regulations generated by the virus.

In Phase 2, when we weren't sure how long our
hibernation would last, I did feel compelled to
tackle those chores I seldom had time to do-like
closet cleaning and learning to make my own bread.

By Phase 3, when it was clear we weren't going
any place any time soon, I felt wonderfully free.
I stopped wearing make-up, coloring my hair,
and succumbed to sweat pants and bedroom slippers.

In Phase 4, I worked on my new book in the a.m.,
then binged a movie or television series in the
afternoon. My customers picked up their Mary
Kay Cosmetics on the porch and left me checks.

I couldn't hold training classes or meetings in
person, so Zoom became my best friend. I was
still in touch with the world without the world
actually entering my space. Life was **so good**!

I guess my life today could be called Phase 5.
I have one reluctant foot in the world and one still
clinging to the dream of that enticing *time picnic,* as
voices in my head whisper, "Maybe it's time to retire."

2022

Around And Around We Go

When the Corona Virus reared its ugly head, everything shut down for two weeks, we thought. So, we all rushed headlong into cleaning closets, organizing our households.

Two weeks became two months, six months, summer, fall, winter, and 2020 disappeared, without family birthdays or Christmas or fun. We became afraid to read the local obituaries.

2021 dawned with hope. Vaccinated now, we tiptoed out of our over-organized houses for maskless lunches with friends. Encouraged, we brazenly grocery-shopped without gloves.

Then, Wham! Bam! We fooled you, Ma'am! Covid returned in coats of many colors, still out to get us, defying our magic vaccines, sending us back inside our houses.

Another summer, fall, winter, and 2021 also disappeared, amidst booster shots and fears. We ventured out more, hugged our family, but there was no real peace in *Happy Valley*.

Now a new year dawns, to fresh-faced expectations, but pandemic life has taught us to be wary. Already, toilet paper is scarce once more, and those closets need cleaning **again.**

February, 2022

America's Grand Reopening What Happens Next??

I pull into a parking place near the restaurant and just sit there, feeling my heartbeat quicken. I've had my vaccine. So has my friend. There is little or no risk to a simple lunch but I can't deny the apprehension.

That was my reaction to my first venture out for a social event after Covid. The lunch was fine. My friend and I laughed about our fear of being out in a clean, socially-distanced restaurant. We'd gotten used to going to the grocery store, post office, and pharmacy in mask and gloves. Removing the mask left us feeling vulnerable, naked. Since then, I've braved a couple more lunches out, and no longer have a near-panic attack in the parking lot. I suspect I'm not the only one inching my way into the world with some reluctance.

As I talk with friends and family, I find many of them changed after a year of forced isolation. My son-in-law and daughter-in-law, have each questioned their job choices and made the difficult decision to change professions in middle age. My son, who lost his job at the beginning of the pandemic, and was out of work for a year, has reinvented himself and is building a new career which brings him joy instead of stress-related indigestion. My daughter has been doing her job from home, and hopes never to return to commuting to a crowded office. Friends have shared similar stories.

There are things we will never take for granted again…full shelves in grocery stores and the people who stock them; hair-cuts, manicures, dentist and doctor appointments; kids going to school and the teachers who are always there for them; movie theatres, remember those? I think we have also come to appreciate time with our families-dinners, game nights, holidays-simple things we never thought we would lose.

I hope we are coming out of the pandemic with a clearer awareness of our own blindness to prejudice and racism, as well as the knowledge that the democracy we thought was forever, is fragile, endangered. We watched a man being murdered in front of our eyes by the police who are supposed to be there to keep us safe. We experienced the horror of an attack on the seat of our government-not by foreign terrorists-but by our fellow citizens. Now we're watching the white-washing of that insurrection by the very people elected to defend those institutions. White supremacy is on the rise. We're seeing laws passed around the country that are deliberately designed to limit or curtail voting for large groups of people-the young, the elderly, black and brown citizens.

A sliver of light peeped through this week as Juneteenth was declared a national holiday, one-hundred-fifty-eight-years after the Emancipation Proclamation was signed by Abraham Lincoln. In the audience for the signing was ninety-five-year-old Opal Lee. At the age of twelve, she and her family barely escaped with their lives when their newly-purchased home in Galveston, Texas, was vandalized and burned to the ground by their white neighbors. The incident never appeared in the news and no one was ever arrested.

Opal grew up to become a teacher who campaigned and marched in support of this holiday for forty years. Each year, on June 19, she would walk two and a half miles in commemoration of the two and a half years it took for the news of the Emancipation Proclamation to reach slaves in Texas. In 2020, at age ninety-four, she and a group of supporters walked for weeks from Ft. Worth, Texas to Washington, D. C. to deliver 1.5 million signatures, again requesting Juneteenth be declared a national holiday. As President Biden signed the proclamation this week, he honored her as the "Grandmother of Juneteenth."

So what happens now, as the country continues to open-up and we restart our lives? I don't know, but I do believe most of us are different, and our lives will be different. Will they be better? I can only hope so.

Our New World

The coronavirus villain in this strange fairy tale is elusive, resilient, and deadly. It has taken control of our lives, locked us behind our doors. It has stolen friends and loved ones from us. We are forever changed.

We will never walk into a movie theatre, restaurant or department store without feeling anxious when we hear someone cough.

We will never again take for granted full shelves in grocery stores or the workers who keep those shelves filled.

We will have more respect for the skilled educators who teach and guide our children.

We will be more grateful for our jobs, even boring ones, that allow us to pay the rent and the electric bill.

We will appreciate being able to go to our doctor or dentist, get a haircut or manicure.

We will elevate all of those health care workers to super hero status along with Wonder Woman and the Avengers.

I would like to think we will emerge from this darkness more enlightened, more compassionate, and more determined to contribute something worthwhile to our new world.

I hope we will be more aware of the "haves" and "have nots," and become activists for equality in housing, in employment, in health care.

I hope we will finally decide that our first responders-teachers, police, firefighters, nurses -deserve to earn more money than baseball players.

I hope we will remember what clear skies look like and clean air smells like and join with the rest of the world in one last attempt to save our planet.

I hope we will all agree that science trumps conspiracy theories and refuse to be taken in by ignorance or misinformation.

I hope we will embrace the blessing of more time with our families and slow our lives enough to continue to play games and tell stories together.

I hope we will heal from the losses with stronger empathy and caring for all people.

Spring's Glorious Entrance

(3-Stanza Tanka)

Humming-birds hover.
Droplets nest on tender leaves.
Grass sheds it's brown shroud.
Buds burst into fragrant blooms.
Daffodils dance on strong legs.

Squirrels search for lost nuts.
A doe shows off her new fawn.
Mama birds guard eggs.
Rains awaken winter fields.
Pollen floats on winds of change.

Windows open wide.
House cleaning madness begins.
Baseballs replace books.
Giggles echo down the block.
Grill-masters dust off aprons.

Part 10

Always Leave 'Em Laughin'

Been There - Done That
Happy Dance!

I Often Wonder

Where the *land of lost dryer socks* is located.

Why I feel 60 on the inside and look 80 on the outside.

Why mac and cheese is much more comforting than broccoli.

How the birds decide who will be the lead in the V formation.

Why my neighbor's chickens poop on my side-walk.

What awful thing I did to deserve a neighbor with chickens.

Why I recall events from high school, but can't remember last week.

Why the pain never goes away when you lose someone you love.

Whether Customer Service puts us on hold, then goes to lunch.

Why everyone doesn't realize my grandchildren are perfect.

Why little lizards no longer have wings.

What the correct order of the Star Wars movies is.

Why I wonder about so many silly things.

The Summertime Open-Toed Shoe Pledge

As a member of the Sophisticated Woman Sisterhood, I pledge to follow these rules when wearing sandals and other open-toed shoes:

- I promise to always wear sandals that fit. My toes will not hang over and drag the ground, nor will my heels spill over the backs. AND the sides and top of my feet will not pudge out between the straps.

- I will go polish-free or vow to keep the polish fresh, intact, and chip-free. I will not just touch up my big toe. I promise to go to my nail salon at least once a season and have a real pedicure.

- Between pedicures, I will sand down any mounds of skin before they turn hard and yellow. I will shave the hairs off my big toe. I will not live in corn denial. Rather, I will lean on my good friend, Dr. Scholl's.

- If a strap breaks, I will not duct-tape, pin, glue, or tuck it back into place, hoping it will stay. I will have my shoe repaired or toss it.

- I will resist the urge to buy jelly shoes at Payless for the low, low price of $4.99, even if my feet are small enough to fit into the kids' sizes. This is out of concern for my safety and the safety of others. No one can walk properly when standing in a pool of sweat. I would hate to take someone down with me as I fall and break an ankle.

- I will take my toe ring off toward the end of the day if my toes swell and begin to look like Vienna sausages.

- I promise to throw away any white/off-white sandals that show signs of wear. Nothing is tackier than dirty white sandals!

- I am headed to my closet right now with a trash bag.

Shoe Shock

Did you know shoes multiply, like rabbits?
You start out with some sturdy Birkenstocks and maybe a pair
of Capezio heels. The next thing you know your closet is overflowing
with pink ballet slippers plus six pairs of multi-colored tennis shoes.

My mother had the worst case of shoe proliferation ever diagnosed.
I blame it on the cold WV climate. All that snuggling in the winter
resulted in multiples of pastel spring sandals and flirty jelly flip-flops.
We unearthed two-hundred pairs from closets and under beds.

Sadly, the inbreeding results in symptoms of instability. Shoes wander
off, but never in pairs, so you venture out to work in one brown loafer
and one chocolate flat. After my last move, I unpacked shoes I'd never
seen before. I have an unproven but logical theory…space aliens.

I applied for a grant to study this footwear phenomenon, deciding it could
be my lasting contribution to society. So far, my only response was a
happy face emoji. I assumed multiplying shoes would trigger concern,
but Russian meddling in our elections stole my air time.

WHY GOD MADE MOTHERS
(AS EXPLAINED BY THIRD GRADERS.)

Why Did God Make Mothers?

Mostly to clean the house and she knows where the scotch tape is.

How Did God Make Mothers?

Magic, plus super powers, and a lot of stirring.

What Ingredients Are Mothers Made Of?

Clouds, angel hair, everything nice in the world, and one dab of mean.

Why Did You Get Your Mother And Not Some Other Mom?

We're related.

What Kind Of Little Girl Was Your Mom?

My guess would be pretty bossy.

THE GIFTS REAL MOMS WOULD LIKE FOR MOTHER'S DAY

A pair of legs that don't ache.

Ams strong enough to pull my screaming child out of the candy aisle.

A waist. I lost mine somewhere in the sixth month of my pregnancy.

Fingerprint resistant windows and walls.

A refrigerator with a secret compartment where I can hide to talk on the phone.

A television that doesn't broadcast any programs with talking animals.

A recording of Tibetan monks chanting, "Wash your hands," and "Don't hit your brother."

A talking doll that says, "Yes, Mommy!" to boost my parental confidence.

Enough time to brush my teeth and comb my hair in the same morning.

The luxury of eating food warmer than room temperature.

A law declaring ketchup and ranch dressing vegetables.

A suggestion for coercing kids to help around the house without demanding payment.

Some writing materials. I'm composing this on a receipt with my son's red crayon.

I would gladly give up all these gifts for a world where we all have jobs, children are safe in school and we can all respect each other.

SIGNED: *Every Mom*

Mom's Revenge

When I'm an old lady, I'll live with each kid.
I'll bring so much happiness-just as they did.
I want to pay back all the joy they've provided,
returning each deed. They'll be so excited!

(When I'm an old lady and live with my kids.)

I'll write on the wall with reds, greens and blues.
I'll bounce on the furniture, wearing my shoes.
I'll drink from the carton, then leave it out.
I'll stuff all the toilets. Oh, how they'll shout!

When they're on the phone and just out of reach,
I'll get into things like sugar and bleach.
They'll snap their fingers, then shake their heads,
and proclaim loudly, "Early to bed!"

(When I'm an old lady and live with my kids.)

When they cook dinner and call me to eat.
I'll not eat my green beans, salad or meat.
I'll gag on my okra, spill milk on the table.
When they get angry, I'll run, if I'm able.

I'll hog the TV, through channels I'll click.
I'll cross both my eyes, to see if they stick.
I'll take off my socks and throw one away,
then play in the mud 'til end of the day.

(When I'm an old lady and live with my kids.)

I'll creep into bed with one muddy sock,
close both eyes tightly when I hear them knock.
My kid will look down with a smile slowly creeping,
and say with a sigh, "She's so sweet when she's sleeping."

Lively Limericks

Wedding Night Lament

There once was a young man named Fred,
who next day was going to wed.
The clock didn't chime,
to get there in time,
so now he's alone in his bed.

Premonition

A round orange head smiles from post.
No legs attached, an eerie ghost.
There's noise by the gate.
He senses his fate.
It's cold pumpkin soup with cheese toast.

Travel Phobia

There once was a lady from Spain
who chose not to travel by plane.
She said, "It's not fair,
to be in the air,
with people who act quite insane."

OOPS!

There once was a cricket named Don,
who liked to hide out in the john.
One day he forgot
to lock down his spot.
One flush and now Donny's long gone.

Invasion

There once was a little green frog,
who lived in a cool woodsy bog.
Tourists descended.
His peace was ended.
He barely escaped, at a jog.

Merry Haiku Christmas

Find the perfect tree.
Drag it home through waist-high snow.
A country Christmas.

Window panes glisten.
Carols fill the silent night.
Wish peace could linger.

Dashing through the mall,
with a list that's two miles long.
Christmas Eve nightmare!

Christmas colors shine
We love their diversity.
Why not in people?

Christmas is giving
of love, of gifts, of ourselves.
Make it last all year.

You better be good.
Elf on the shelf is watching.
Let's blindfold that guy!

A Change In Christmas Plans

Martha Stewart will not be dining with us this Christmas. Since Ms. Stewart had another engagement, I've deviated slightly from her suggestions.

Our sidewalk will not be lined with homemade, paper bag luminaries. After a trial run, it was decided, no matter how cleverly done, rows of flaming lunch sacks do not have the desired welcoming effect.

You will also notice the entry hall is not decorated with swags of holly and pine, as suggested by Ms. Stewart. Instead, I've gotten grand-dog, Daisy, involved in the decorating by having her track in colorful autumn leaves from the yard. The mud was her own idea.

The dining table will not be covered with expensive linens, fancy china, or crystal goblets. If possible, we will use dishes that match and everyone will get a fork. Our centerpiece will not be a tower of fresh fruit and flowers. Instead, we will be displaying a hedgehog-like decoration, handcrafted by granddaughters, Adaline, and Emma, from the finest construction paper. The artists assure me it is a Christmas tree.

We will be dining fashionably late. Grandson, Zachary, will entertain you with magic tricks while you wait. As accompaniment, I will play a recording of tribal drumming. If the tribal drumming sounds suspiciously like a frozen ham in a clothes dryer, it is a mere coincidence.

We toyed with the idea of ringing a dainty silver bell to announce the start of our feast. In the end, we chose to keep our traditional method. We've also decided against a formal seating arrangement. When the smoke alarm sounds, please gather around the table. Sit wherever you like.

Now, I know you've seen pictures of a person carving the ham in front of a crowd of appreciative onlookers. This will not occur at our dinner. For safety reasons, the ham will be carved in a private ceremony. Do not, under any circumstances, enter the kitchen. I have an electric knife. The ham is unarmed. It stands to reason, I will eventually prevail. When I do, we will eat.

I would like to remind diners that *passing the rolls* is not a football play. Before I forget, there is one last change. Instead of offering a choice of twelve different scrumptious desserts, we will be serving the traditional pumpkin pie, garnished with whipped cream and very possibly decorated with tiny grandchildren fingerprints.

Merry Christmas Dinner!!

'TWAS THE WEEK AFTER CHRISTMAS

'Twas the week after Christmas, all through the house,
nothing would fit, not even a blouse.
The cookies I'd nibbled, the eggnog I'd taste,
at holiday parties, had gone to my waist.

I recall the marvelous meals all prepared,
the gravies and sauces, the beef nicely rared.
The wine and the rum balls, the bread and the cheese,
the way I did not say, "Take it away, please!"

Away with the last of the sour cream dip.
Get rid of the fruitcake, all crackers and chips.
Each bite of food that I like must be banished,
'til all of the extra ounces have vanished.

I won't have a cookie, not even a lick.
From now on, I'll chew on a celery stick.
I won't eat hot biscuits or cornbread or pie.
I'll munch on a carrot and quietly cry.

I'm hungry, I'm lonesome, and life is a bore,
but isn't that what January is for?
Unable to laugh, no longer a riot,
Happy New Year to all, and to all a good diet.

I Used To...

I used to wear high heels and flashy earrings
for theatre evenings and dinners in candle-lit cafes.
Midnight wasn't my bedtime.
It was the beginning of more fun.

Now I prefer my sweats, tennis shoes,
no make-up, while Door Dash delivers dinner,
which is consumed in my easy chair,
watching a Netflix romcom or Hallmark mystery.

I used to love traveling around the world,
hiking majestic mountains, swimming nude
in cascading waterfalls, sleeping under the stars
with my handsome, adventurous husband.

Now I do water therapy twice a week for my
aging back, see the chiropractor more often than
my grandkids, and daily, repeat that adage,
"Any day you can get out of bed is a good day!"

I used to count calories religiously, passing up
favorites like mac and cheese or pizza,
for broccoli, baked chicken and sugar-free
lime jello with shredded carrots.

How did that woman survive those lean years?
Now I celebrate *Mac and Cheese Friday* and
Any Day Pizza Lunch. I also faithfully adhere
to the sugarholic's rule, "Eat your dessert first!"

I used to adore long lunches with girlfriends, and
juicy gossip about whoever didn't show up that day.
Now the conversations are about doctors, Botox,
and whether to let our hair go gray.

By now, I'm sure you're feeling pity for the old
woman who had to give up all those fun adventures.
Don't be sorry! Been there, done that, and still have a
rich cache of memories, souvenirs, and some scars.

Today, happiness is all of those lazy, decadent things,
plus the fun of watching my children morph into healthy,
productive adults, and my grandkids experience the world.
Life is good! I flaunt the t'shirt proclaiming it.

Would I like to go back, do it all again? Nope!
(Well, maybe the nude swimming with my sexy man.)

Other Books by Sharon Canfield Dorsey

Children's Literature:

Revolt of the Teacups (October 2017)

Buddy and Ballerina Save the Library (November 2018)

Herman the Hermit Crab: and The Mystery Of The Big Black, Shiny Thing (September 2016)

Buddy the Bookworm: Rescues the Doomed Books (December 2018)

Poetry:

Walk with Me: The Poetry of Sharon Canfield Dorsey (November, 2020)

Tapestry: The Poems of Sharon Canfield Dorsey (August 2016)

Non-Fiction:

The Move: How to Get Rid of All that Stuff and Downsize (June 2024)

Begin Somewhere: (December 2023)

Road Trip: A Love Letter to America (June 2023)

Twenty-Four Months That Changed the World: and Us (July 2022)

Road Trippin': In the Era of COVID-19 (September 2020)

Memoir:

Daughter of the Mountains: A Memoir (August 2017)

Anthologies:

Captured Moments: The Poetry Anthology of the James City Poets (November 2017)

The Journal: The Writers Guild of Virginia (various)

About the Author

SHARON CANFIELD DORSEY is an award-winning author and poet who has published fiction, non-fiction, juvenile fiction, and poetry in magazines, newspapers, and journals.

She is a Past Vice President of the Poetry Society of VA, a member of the Writer's Guild of VA, and the National League of American Pen Women. She has received awards from Christopher Newport University, Poetry Society of Virginia, Gulf Coast Writer's Association, NLAPW, and Chesapeake Bay Writers. Her poetry was selected in an areawide contest to be printed on the sidewalks of her hometown, Williamsburg, VA. Sharon has published thirteen books.

She is a Senior Sales Director of forty-two years with Mary Kay Cosmetics; Mom to son, Steven (Amy), and daughter, Shannon (AJ); Grandmother to Adaline, Emma and Zachary.

Support Your Local Authors

DID YOU KNOW…when you purchase a book you start a chain reaction that keeps print books and starving authors alive and well?

You encourage an author-maybe a brand-new author-to keep on sharing their important stories. Our royalty checks allow us to buy more printer ink and reams of white paper (much of which winds up crumpled under the computer desk as we perfect those magic words.)

You also encourage publishers to sign more authors whose unique stories might not otherwise be read.

When readers purchase books, that encourages the establishment of new publishing companies, who publish more new authors, who inspire and brighten our lives.

The company that publishes my books, High Tide Publications, is a small, woman-owned enterprise that is dedicated to the author over fifty, which is an under-served and often ignored market. When you purchase High Tide books, you are helping authors like me get our stories into the world. You will be much appreciated!

www.ingramcontent.com/pod-product-compliance
Lightning Source LLC
Chambersburg PA
CBHW070447050426
42451CB00015B/3374